TEACHER'S PET PUBLICATIONS

LITPLAN TEACHER PACK
for
Their Eyes Were Watching God
based on the book by
Zora Neale Hurston

Written by
Barbara M. Linde, MA Ed.

© 1995 Teacher's Pet Publications
All Rights Reserved

This **LitPlan** for Zora Neal Hurston's
Their Eyes Were Watching God
has been brought to you by Teacher's Pet Publications, Inc.

Copyright Teacher's Pet Publications 1995
11504 Hammock Point
Berlin MD 21811

Only the student materials in this unit plan (such as worksheets,
study questions, puzzles, and tests) may be reproduced multiple times
for use in the purchaser's classroom.

For any additional copyright questions,
contact Teacher's Pet Publications.

www.tpet.com

NOTE: Several pages have been left blank in this LitPlan.
This was done on purpose to make the divider pages
print on the right-hand page when printing two-sided.
If you are printing one-sided, just ignore the extra pages.

TABLE OF CONTENTS - *Their Eyes Were Watching God*

Introduction	5
Unit Objectives	7
Unit Outline	8
Reading Assignment Sheet	9
Study Questions	13
Quiz/Study Questions (Multiple Choice)	23
Pre-Reading Vocabulary Worksheets	39
Lesson One (Introductory Lesson)	55
Nonfiction Assignment Sheet	59
Oral Reading Evaluation Form	61
Writing Assignment 1	63
Writing Evaluation Form	64
Writing Assignment 2	67
Extra Writing Assignments/Discussion ?s	69
Writing Assignment 3	73
Vocabulary Review Activities	74
Unit Review Activities	77
Unit Tests	83
Unit Resource Materials	123
Vocabulary Resource Materials	143

A FEW NOTES ABOUT THE AUTHOR
ZORA NEALE HURSTON

HURSTON, Zora Neale (1903 ?-1960) Zora Neale Hurston was born in Eatonville, Florida, on January 7, 1901 (some say 1903.) She wrote four novels as well as two books of black mythology, legends, and folklore.

Hurston traveled with a theater company in her teenage years and then attended Barnard College, where she studied anthropology. During several years of field service after college she studied African American folklore in her native Florida. One result of this study was the book *Mules and Men* (1935), a collection of folklore presented within the framework of a unifying narrative.

Hurston's background was also reflected in her novels, most of which incorporated elements of folklore to some degree. *Their Eyes Were Watching God* (1937), which was widely praised as her finest novel, told the story of a young black woman's growth toward self-awareness and independence. Hurston's other novels were *Jonah's Gourd Vine* (1934), the tale of a black preacher; the allegorical *Moses, Man of the Mountain* (1939), and *Seraph on the Suanee* (1948).

In the early 1930s Hurston became involved in the Harlem Renaissance movement, where she represented the black experience of the rural South. Her work subsequently influenced Toni Morrison, Ralph Ellison, and other black authors. She also wrote *Tell My Horse* (1938), which was originally published as *Voodoo Gods: An Inquiry into Native Myths and Magic in Jamaica and Haiti*. *Dust Tracks on a Road* (1942), was her autobiography. Her book *I Love Myself When I Am Laughing* was published posthumously in 1979. It contained a selections of stories, novels, and essays. She died on January 28, 1960, in Fort Pierce, Florida.

Courtesy of Compton's Learning Company

INTRODUCTION

This unit has been designed to develop students' reading, writing, thinking, listening and speaking skills through exercises and activities related to *Their Eyes Were Watching God* by Zora Neale Hurston. It includes nineteen lessons, supported by extra resource materials.

The **introductory lesson** introduces students to one main theme of the novel (Janie's development through a bulletin board activity. Following the introductory activity, students are given an explanation of how the activity relates to the book they are about to read.

The **reading assignments** are approximately thirty pages each; some are a little shorter while others are a little longer. Students have approximately 15 minutes of pre-reading work to do prior to each reading assignment. This pre-reading work involves reviewing the study questions for the assignment and doing some vocabulary work for 8 to 10 vocabulary words they will encounter in their reading.

The **study guide questions** are fact-based questions; students can find the answers to these questions right in the text. These questions come in two formats: short answer or multiple choice. The best use of these materials is probably to use the short answer version of the questions as study guides for students (since answers will be more complete), and to use the multiple choice version for occasional quizzes. It might be a good idea to make transparencies of your answer keys for the overhead projector.

The **vocabulary work** is intended to enrich students' vocabularies as well as to aid in the students' understanding of the book. Prior to each reading assignment, students will complete a two-part worksheet for approximately 8 to 10 vocabulary words in the upcoming reading assignment. Part I focuses on students' use of general knowledge and contextual clues by giving the sentence in which the word appears in the text. Students are then to write down what they think the words mean based on the words' usage. Part II gives students dictionary definitions of the words and has them match the words to the correct definitions based on the words' contextual usage. Students should then have an understanding of the words when they meet them in the text.

After each reading assignment, students will go back and formulate answers for the study guide questions. Discussion of these questions serves as a **review** of the most important events and ideas presented in the reading assignments.

After students complete extra discussion questions, there is a **vocabulary review** lesson which pulls together all of the separate vocabulary lists for the reading assignments and gives students a review of all of the words they have studied.

Following the reading of the book, two lessons are devoted to the **extra discussion questions/writing assignments**. These questions focus on interpretation, critical analysis and personal response, employing a variety of thinking skills and adding to the students' understanding of the novel. These questions are done as a **group activity**. Using the information they have acquired so far through individual work and class discussions, students get together to further examine the text and to brainstorm ideas relating to the themes of the novel.

The group activity is followed by a **reports and discussion** session in which the groups share their ideas about the book with the entire class; thus, the entire class gets exposed to many different ideas regarding the themes and events of the book.

There are three **writing assignments** in this unit, each with the purpose of informing, persuading, or having students express personal opinions. The first assignment is to **inform**: students will write a public service announcement outlining what to do if there is a hurricane. The second assignment is to **persuade**: students will take the role of a sales representative and make a presentation to Joe Starks, convincing him to stock their product in his store. The third assignment is to express a personal **opinion**: students will add a chapter to the novel, detailing what they think should happen next in Janie's life.

In addition, there is a **nonfiction reading assignment**. Students are required to read a piece of nonfiction related in some way to *Their Eyes Were Watching God*

After reading their nonfiction pieces, students will fill out a worksheet on which they answer questions regarding facts, interpretation, criticism, and personal opinions. During one class period, students make **oral presentations** about the nonfiction pieces they have read. This not only exposes all students to a wealth of information, it also gives students the opportunity to practice **public speaking**.

The **review lesson** pulls together all of the aspects of the unit. The teacher is given four or five choices of activities or games to use which all serve the same basic function of reviewing all of the information presented in the unit.

The **unit test** comes in two formats: all multiple choice-matching-true/false or with a mixture of matching, short answer, and composition. As a convenience, two different tests for each format have been included.

There are additional **support materials** included with this unit. The **resource section** includes suggestions for an in-class library, crossword and word search puzzles related to the novel, and extra vocabulary worksheets. There is a list of **bulletin board ideas** which gives the teacher suggestions for bulletin boards to go along with this unit. In addition, there is a list of **extra class activities** the teacher could choose from to enhance the unit or as a substitution for an exercise the teacher might feel is inappropriate for his/her class. **Answer keys** are located directly after the **reproducible student materials** throughout the unit. The student materials may be reproduced for use in the teacher's classroom without infringement of copyrights. No other portion of this unit may be reproduced without the written consent of Teacher's Pet Publications, Inc.

UNIT OBJECTIVES *Their Eyes Were Watching God*

1. Through reading *Their Eyes Were Watching God,* students will analyze characters and their situations to better understand the themes of the novel.

2. Students will demonstrate their understanding of the text on four levels: factual, interpretive, critical, and personal.

3. Students will practice reading aloud and silently to improve their skills in each area.

4. Students will enrich their vocabularies and improve their understanding of the autobiography through the vocabulary lessons prepared for use in conjunction with it.

5. Students will answer questions to demonstrate their knowledge and understanding of the main events and characters in *Their Eyes Were Watching God.*

6. Students will practice writing through a variety of writing assignments.

7. The writing assignments in this are geared to several purposes:
    a. To check the students' reading comprehension
    b. To make students think about the ideas presented by the novel
    c. To make students put those ideas into perspective
    d. To encourage critical and logical thinking
    e. To provide the opportunity to practice good grammar and improve students' use of the English language.

8. Students will read aloud, report, and participate in large and small group discussions to improve their public speaking and personal interaction skills.

UNIT OUTLINE - *Their Eyes Were Watching God*

1 Unit Intro PV 1-4	2 Read 1-4 Study ?s 1-4	3 PVR 5-6 Oral Reading Evaluation	4 Quiz 1-6 PVR 7-11	5 Writing Assignment 1
6 Study ?s 7-11 PVR 12-15	7 Study ?s 12-15 PVR 16-18	8 Study ?s 16-18 Writing Assignment 2	9 Writing Conferences	10 PVR 19-20 Study ?s 19-20
11 Extra Discusson ?s	12 Writing Assignment 3	13 Library	14 Vocab Review	15 Group Work
16 Movie/Audio Cassette & Discussion	17 Non-Fiction Assignment	18 Review	19 Test	

Key: P = Preview Study Questions   V = Vocabulary Work   R = Read

READING ASSIGNMENT SHEET
Their Eyes Were Watching God

Date Assigned	Chapters	Complete By
	1-4	
	5-6	
	7-11	
	12-15	
	16-18	
	19-20	

STUDY GUIDE QUESTIONS

SHORT ANSWER STUDY GUIDE QUESTIONS
Their Eyes Were Watching God

Chapters 1-4
1. Who is the main character?
2. What is her situation at the beginning of the novel?
3. What was Janie's most noticeable physical characteristic?
4. Who was Janie's best friend?
5. After Chapter 1, how is the story told?
6. Why did Janie marry Logan Killicks?
7. What was Janie's idea of love before she was married?
8. What happened to Nanny shortly after Janie was married?
9. How did Janies's and Logan's relationship change?
10. What did Janie discover about love?
11. Describe Joe Starks.
12. What did Janie do shortly after she met Joe Starks?

Chapters 5 & 6
1. Who was Joe looking for when he and Janie got to town?
2. What were the two names of the town?
3. What actions did Joe take when he got to town?
4. How did Joe want Janie to look and act?
5. What was the result of Joe's suggestion that the town incorporate and elect a mayor?
6. What was Janie's reaction when Joe said she couldn't make a speech?
7. Which of Joe's innovations was the first in a colored town?
8. How did Joe's position affect Janie's' relationship with other town residents?
9. What was the "rock" against which Janie was battered?
10. What did Joe do about the mule?
11. What happened to Joe and Janie's relationship during the seventh year of their marriage?
12. What was Janie's comment to the men during their conversation about Mrs. Tony?

Short Answer Study Guide Questions *Their Eyes Were Watching God*

Chapters 7-11
1. What was the real reason behind the argument between Joe and Janie that started when she incorrectly cut the plug of tobacco?
2. How did Janie feel after the big argument in the store?
3. What did Janie tell Joe just before he died?
4. What was the only change that people saw in Janie after Joe's funeral?
5. What did Phoeby and the other townspeople think Janie should do?
6. What did Janie think of the idea of remarrying?
7. What did Janie say about mourning and grief?
8. How did Janie meet Tea Cake?
9. Describe Tea Cake.
10. What were the main concerns that Janie had about getting into a relationship with Tea Cake?
11. Why did Tea Cake visit Janie early one morning?
12. What did Tea Cake do that proved his serious intentions toward Janie?

Chapters 12-15
1. How did the townspeople feel about Janie going out with Tea Cake?
2. What was Janie's response when Phoeby talked to her about Tea Cake?
3. Why did Janie want to sell the store?
4. Summarize Janie and Tea Cake's wedding.
5. What did Janie discover one morning about a week after she was married?
6. What did Janie tell Tea Cake when he returned home after having spent her money?
7. How did Tea Cake get the money back?
8. Where did Janie and Tea Cake go, and why?

Short Answer Study Guide Questions *Their Eyes Were Watching God*

Chapters 12-15 continued
9. Describe the muck.
10. How did Janie feel about her life with Tea Cake?
11. Why did Janie start going out to pick beans?
12. Describe the incident with Nunkie.

Chapters 16-18
1. Describe Mrs. Turner and her attitude about Negroes.
2. What did Mrs. Turner propose to Janie, and why?
3. What did Tea Cake do after Mrs. Turner introduced her brother to Janie and Tea Cake, and why?
4. How did the men react to Tea Cake's treatment of Janie?
5. Describe the incident in Mrs. Turner's restaurant.
6. What was Mrs. Turner's reaction to the incident?
7. What caused the Seminoles, and then the animals, to move eastward?
8. Why did some of the people, including Tea Cake and Janie, remain in their houses on the muck?
9. What was Janie's response when Tea Cake asked Janie if she wished she had stayed in her big house, away from dangers such as the hurricane?
10. Describe what was happening when the author used the sentence: "They seemed to be staring at the dark, but their eyes were watching God."
11. What did Janie and Tea Cake do to try and escape from the lake?
12. Describe the incident with the cow and the dog.

Chapters 19-20
1. What did Janie and Tea Cake do after the hurricane was over?
2. What happened in the middle of their fourth week back on the muck?
3. What were Tea Cake's symptoms?
4. What did the doctor tell Janie after he examined Tea Cake?
5. What did Janie do after the doctor left?
6. What did Janie find under Tea Cake's pillow?
7. What did Janie do after she found this?
8. Describe what happened when Tea Cake came back into the house.
9. Describe Janie and Tea Cake's last moments together.
10. What happened at the trial?
11. How did the other men from the muck feel at the trial?
12. What did Janie bring back to Eatonville?

ANSWER KEY: SHORT ANSWER STUDY GUIDE QUESTIONS
Their Eyes Were Watching God

Chapters 1-4

1. Who is the main character?
   The main character is Janie Mae Crawford.

2. What is her situation at the beginning of the novel?
   She is returning home after having been gone for some time.

3. What was Janie's most noticeable physical characteristic?
   She had beautiful, long dark hair.

4. Who was Janie's best friend?
   It was Phoeby Watson.

5. After Chapter 1, how is the story told?
   It is told as a flashback.

6. Why did Janie marry Logan Killicks?
   Her grandmother made her marry him. Nanny was concerned that Janie be taken care of before she (Nanny) died.

7. What was Janie's idea of love before she was married?
   She thought she would grow to love her husband, because husbands and wives always loved each other.

8. What happened to Nanny shortly after Janie was married?
   She died.

9. How did Janies's and Logan's relationship change?
   At first he talked in rhymes and did things for her. Then he told her she had to do more work.

10. What did Janie discover about love?
    She discovered that marriage did not make love.

11. Describe Joe Starks.
    He was citified, stylishly dressed, and had money and ambitions.

12. What did Janie do shortly after she met Joe Starks?
    She left Logan and ran off with Joe Starks.

Chapters 5 & 6
1. Who was Joe looking for when he and Janie got to town?
    He was looking for the mayor.

2. What were the two names of the town?
    It was called West Maitland and Eatonville.

3. What actions did Joe take when he got to town?
    He paid cash for 200 acres of land. He opened a store and a post office. He bought the town's first street lamp. He organized the men and built a road. He had a drainage ditch built.

4. How did Joe want Janie to look and act?
    He wanted her to be "the bell-cow;" to look and act better than the other women.

5. What was the result of Joe's suggestion that the town incorporate and elect a mayor?
    He was elected mayor.

6. What was Janie's reaction when Joe said she couldn't make a speech?
    She felt cold; his remarks took the bloom off things.

7. Which of Joe's innovations was the first in a colored town?
    It was the street lamp.

8. How did Joe's position affect Janie's relationship with other town residents?
    She couldn't get close to most of them. They felt jealous and awestruck.

9. What was the "rock" against which Janie was battered?
    She was frustrated in the store when she had to deal with the math involved in the customers' purchases. Joe said she could do it id she wanted to, and he wanted her to use her privileges.

10. What did Joe do about the mule?
    He bought it so it could stay in the pasture and rest.

11. What happened to Joe and Janie's relationship during the seventh year of their marriage?
    Joe started criticizing Janie. At first she fought back, but she gradually submitted. She learned to keep her thoughts to herself.

12. What was Janie's comment to the men during their conversation about Mrs. Tony?
    She said God told her how surprised he was that they turned out so smart after he made them different than women, and that they would be surprised if they ever found out they didn't know half as much about women as they thought.

Chapters 7-11

1. What was the real reason behind the argument between Joe and Janie that started when she incorrectly cut the plug of tobacco?
   Joe realized he wasn't as young as he used to be. He started picking on Janie because of his fear about his own aging.

2. How did Janie feel after the big argument in the store?
   She was very upset and cried often.

3. What did Janie tell Joe just before he died?
   She told him he really didn't know her, that she had a lot of sympathy but he would never let her use it.

4. What was the only change that people saw in Janie after Joe's funeral?
   She stopped wearing the headrags.

5. What did Phoeby and the other townspeople think Janie should do?
   They thought she should remarry.

6. What did Janie think of the idea of remarrying?
   She didn't want to. She loved her new freedom.

7. What did Janie say about mourning and grief?
   She said mourning shouldn't last any longer than grief.

8. How did Janie meet Tea Cake?
   He came into the store and started talking to her.

9. Describe Tea Cake.
   He was tall and lean. He had full, lazy eyes. He joked and laughed a lot.

10. What were the main concerns that Janie had about getting into a relationship with Tea Cake?
    He was about twelve years younger than she was. He didn't look like he had much money. She wasn't sure his intentions were serious or honorable.

11. Why did Tea Cake visit Janie early one morning?
    He wanted to tell her his daytime thoughts. Janie still had doubts about the seriousness of his intentions, so he was attempting to prove to her that he was serious about her.

12. What did Tea Cake do that proved his serious intentions toward Janie?
    He brought her strawberries in the morning so she could listen to his daytime thoughts. He invited her to the big Sunday School picnic.

Chapters 12-15

1. How did the townspeople feel about Janie going out with Tea Cake?
   They thought he was trying to take advantage of her.

2. What was Janie's response when Phoeby talked to her about Tea Cake?
   She said she had always wanted to go and do the things that she was doing with Tea Cake, but that Joe wouldn't let her.

3. Why did Janie want to sell the store?
   She planned to marry Tea Cake. She didn't want people comparing him to Joe.

4. Summarize Janie and Tea Cake's wedding.
   Janie took the train to Jacksonville, wearing her new blue satin dress. Tea Cake met her at the train and took her to the preacher's house, where they got married.

5. What did Janie discover one morning about a week after she was married?
   She woke up and discovered that Tea Cake had taken her $200 and left their room before she woke up.

6. What did Janie tell Tea Cake when he returned home after having spent her money?
   She told him she intended to partake of everything with him, and if he ever went off and had fun without her again, she would kill him.

7. How did Tea Cake get the money back?
   He gambled and won $322.00.

8. Where did Janie and Tea Cake go, and why?
   They went to the Everglades, "de muck," to pick beans.

9. Describe the muck.
   It was a section of the Everglades near Clewiston and Belle Glade where sugar cane, string beans, and tomatoes were raised.

10. How did Janie feel about her life with Tea Cake?
    She enjoyed the work and the social life.

11. Why did Janie start going out to pick beans?
    Teacake asked her to, because he missed her during the day.

12. Describe the incident with Nunkie.
    Nunkie was making a play for Tea Cake. Janie found them struggling in one of the cane rows, and confronted them. When they got back to their house they wrestled, then finally made up. The next morning, Tea Cake reassured Janie that she was the only woman in whom he was interested.

Chapters 16-18

1. Describe Mrs. Turner and her attitude about Negroes.
   Mrs. Turner was light-skinned, with Caucasian features. She prided herself on not looking like the other Negroes. She did not like black Negroes, and thought herself better than them.

2. What did Mrs. Turner propose to Janie, and why?
   Mrs. Turner thought Janie was too fine-featured to be married to a man as black as Tea Cake. She wanted to introduce Janie to her brother.

3. What did Tea Cake do after Mrs. Turner introduced her brother to Janie and Tea Cake, and why?
   He whipped Janie to show that he was still in possession of her. He wanted to show the Turners that he was still the boss.

4. How did the men react to Tea Cake's treatment of Janie?
   They congratulated him because all of Janie's bruises were visible, which meant she did not fight back. They said their wives would have fought and screamed.

5. Describe the incident in Mrs. Turner's restaurant.
    The men were all eating at the restaurant when Serrent and Coodemay came in drunk. The place was full, so Coodemay tried to shove Sop-de-Bottom out of his chair. Tea Cake tried to take Coodemay and Serrent out of the restaurant, which started a general melee. The inside of the restaurant was in a shambles by the time the fight was over.

6. What was Mrs. Turner's reaction to the incident?
    She told her husband she wanted to move back to Miami.

7. What caused the Seminoles, and then the animals, to move eastward?
    A hurricane was coming.

8. Why did some of the people, including Tea Cake and Janie, remain in their houses on the muck?
    They thought they were safe because of the dike. They also thought the boss-man would be able to stop the hurricane by morning.

9. What was Janie's response when Tea Cake asked Janie if she wished she had stayed in her big house, away from dangers such as the hurricane?
    She said when she was with her husband in a storm, she didn't think she would die until her time came, and that she was happy being with Tea Cake.

10. Describe what was happening when the author used the sentence: "They seemed to be staring at the dark, but their eyes were watching God."
    The people who had not left for higher ground were staring out at the fury of the hurricane.

11. What did Janie and Tea Cake do to try and escape from the lake?
    They started walking and swimming toward the high road that went to Palm Beach.

12. Describe the incident with the cow and the dog.
    Janie had grabbed onto a piece of roofing to use to cover Tea Cake. The wind came up and blew her and the roofing into the water. A cow was swimming by, and Tea Cake told her to grab its tail. There was a dog on the cow's back. The dog advanced towards Janie. Tea Cake jumped in the water and fought the dog. The dog bit him before he was able to kill it.

Chapters 19-20
1. What did Janie and Tea Cake do after the hurricane was over?
    After a few days, they went back to the muck and were reunited with many of their old friends.

2. What happened in the middle of their fourth week back on the muck?
   Tea Cake came home complaining of a headache.

3. What were Tea Cake's symptoms?
   He had a headache and a fever, his throat was closed up, and he couldn't swallow anything, not even water.

4. What did the doctor tell Janie when he came to see Tea Cake?
   He said Tea Cake had rabies, and that he had almost no chance to recover.

5. What did Janie do after the doctor left?
   She went outside and looked up at the sky. She wondered if God was noticing what was going on, and if he had intentionally caused this problem for her and Tea Cake.

6. What did Janie find under Tea Cake's pillow?
   She found his pistol, with three full chambers.

7. What did Janie do after she found this?
   When Tea Cake went outside, she whirled the cylinder so the three empty chambers would snap first. Then she readied the rifle and put it in a corner of the kitchen.

8. Describe what happened when Tea Cake came back into the house.
   He was in a delirious rage and aimed the pistol at Janie. After he shot once, Janie readied the rifle. He discharged the other two empty cylinders, then got ready to shoot again. Janie and Tea Cake shot at the same time, and Janie shot and killed Tea Cake.

9. Describe Janie and Tea Cake's last moments together.
   Janie held Tea Cake in her arms and wept and silently thanked him for the time they had together. Tea Cake bit her on the arm just before he died.

10. What happened at the trial?
    The doctor testified that Janie had acted in self-defense. Janie testified and tried to tell the jury how bad the situation was. She was acquitted.

11. How did the other men from the muck feel at the trial?
    At first they felt that Janie should have been convicted of murder, but they relented after a while.

12. What did Janie bring back to Eatonville?
    She brought the pack of seeds that Tea Cake had wanted to plant.

MULTIPLE CHOICE STUDY GUIDE/QUIZ QUESTIONS *Their Eyes Were Watching God*

Chapters 1-4

1. True or False: The main character's birth name was Janie Logan.
    A. True
    B. False

2. What is the main character's situation at the beginning of the novel?
    A. The main character is dying and reflecting back on life.
    B. The main character is returning home after having been gone for some time.
    C. The main character is writing memoirs.
    D. The main character is talking to a grandchild about life in "the old days."

3. What was Janie's most noticeable physical characteristic?
    A. Her skin was a deep, rich ebony color.
    B. She was six feet tall.
    C. She had long, beautiful dark hair.
    D. She walked with a limp.

4. Who was Janie's best friend?
    A. It was Mae Washburn.
    B. It was Phoeby Watson.
    C. It was Jody Taylor.
    D. It was Mrs. Sterrent.

5. True or False: After Chapter 1, the story is told as a flashback.
    A. True
    B. False

6. Why did Janie marry Logan Killicks?
    A. She wanted his land and his money.
    B. She thought she was pregnant and wanted a father for the baby.
    C. She wanted to get away from her grandmother.
    D. Her grandmother made her marry him for security.

7. True or False: Janie thought she would grow to love her husband, because husbands and wives always loved each other.
    A. True
    B. False

Multiple Choice Study Guide/Quiz Questions *Their Eyes Were Watching God*

Chapters 1-4 continued

8. What happened to Nanny shortly after Janie was married?
   A. She went to Tampa to visit her sister.
   B. She moved in with Janie and Logan.
   C. She died.
   D. She had a stroke and Janie put her in a nursing home.

9. True or False: Logan was mean to Janie at first, but became sweet and loving as time went on.
   A. True
   B. False

10. What did Janie discover about love?
    A. She discovered she was not capable of love.
    B. She discovered she did not like being in love.
    C. She discovered that her initial thoughts about love were correct.
    D. She discovered that marriage did not make love.

11. Which of the following does **not** describe Joe Starks?
    A. He was citified.
    B. He was stylishly dressed
    C. He spoke with a Northern accent.
    D. He had money and ambitions.

12. What did Janie do shortly after she met Joe Starks?
    A. She left Logan and ran off with Joe .
    B. She told Logan he was bothering her?
    C. She told Joe he was the kindest person she had ever met?
    B. She stopped working in the store.

Multiple Choice Study Guide/Quiz Questions *Their Eyes Were Watching God*

Chapters 5 & 6

1. Who was Joe looking for when he and Janie got to town?
    A. He was looking for the real estate agent.
    B. He was looking for the preacher to marry him and Janie.
    C. He was looking for the doctor.
    D. He was looking for the mayor.

2. What were the two names of the town?
    A. It was called East Maitland and Easton.
    B. It was called West Maitland and Eatonville.
    C. It was called Eatontown and South Mainland.
    D. It was called Eatonland and North Mainton.

3. Which of the following is **not** something Joe did when he got to town?
    A. He bought the town's first automobile.
    B. He paid cash for 200 acres of land.
    C. He opened a store and a post office. He bought the town's first street lamp.
    D. He organized the men to build a road and a drainage ditch.

4. True or False: Joe wanted Janie to look and act very modest and unassuming. He didn't want her "putting on airs" and acting better than the other townspeople.
    A. True
    B. False

5. What was the result of Joe's suggestion that the town incorporate and elect a mayor?
    A. The townspeople laughed and said the was getting too sophisticated for them.
    B. The townspeople elected Tony Taylor mayor.
    C. The townspeople elected Joe mayor.
    D. They found out there was a law that a black town had to have a white mayor, so they dropped the idea.

6. What was Janie's reaction when Joe said she couldn't make a speech?
    A. She felt cold; his remarks took the bloom off things.
    B. She was glad, because she didn't want to make a speech.
    TWO CHOICES ONLY

Multiple Choice Study Guide/Quiz Questions *Their Eyes Were Watching God*

Chapters 5-6 continued

7. Which of Joe's innovations was the first in a colored town?
   A. It was running water in all of the houses.
   B. It was the cash register in the store.
   C. It was the telephone in his house.
   D. It was the street lamp.

8. How did Joe's position affect Janie's' relationship with other town residents?
   A. She became "the belle of the ball" and was invited to all of the social functions.
   B. She couldn't get close to most of them. They felt jealous and awestruck.
   C. She became a role model for all of the young girls.
   D. Her popularity helped Joe attract customers to the store and remain as mayor.

9. True or False: Janie was frustrated with trying to do the math required of her in the store.
   A. True
   B. False

10. What did Joe do about the mule?
    A. He killed it.
    B. He sold it to a man who was traveling through town.
    C. He put it out in the woods, hoping it would wander away.
    D. He bought it and gave it a place to rest.

11. What happened to Joe and Janie's relationship during the seventh year of their marriage?
    A. It got better than it ever had been. Joe started complimenting her and buying her gifts.
    B. Janie began making fun of Joe for things he did.
    C. Janie learned to keep her thoughts to herself instead of fighting Joe's criticism.
    D. Janie wanted a divorce but Joe wouldn't let her get one.

12. True or False: Janie told the men they would be surprised if they ever found out they didn't know half as much about women as they thought.
    A. True
    B. False

Multiple Choice Study Guide/Quiz Questions *Their Eyes Were Watching God*
Chapters 7-11

1. What was the real reason behind the argument between Joe and Janie that started with her incorrectly cutting the plug of tobacco?
    A. Joe realized he wasn't as young as he used to be. He started picking on Janie because of his fear about his own aging.
    B. Joe was jealous. He thought she was giving Steve Mixon extra tobacco because she was secretly in love with him.
    C. He was furious because she was losing money for the store.
    D. He liked it that she was helpless and ineffective, because it made him look competent and generous to the customers.

2. Janie was glad she had insulted Joe in front of all of the customers. She told everyone he had it coming.
    A. True
    B. False

3. What did Janie tell Joe just before he died?
    A. She told him she had never really loved him.
    B. She told him she wished he could live forever, because she couldn't imagine life without him.
    C. She told him he really didn't know her, that she had a lot of sympathy but he would never let her use it.
    D. She promised him she would give him the best funeral possible, and that she would keep the store just the way he had it.

4. What was the only change that people saw in Janie after Joe's funeral?
    A. She insisted that people call her "Widow Starks."
    B. She stopped smiling entirely.
    C. She stopped wearing the headrags.
    D. She spent more time in her garden than she had before.

5. What did Phoeby and the other townspeople think Janie should do?
    A. They thought she should run for mayor.
    B. They thought she should sell the store and move to a big city.
    C. They thought she should leave everything just the way it was.
    D. They thought she should remarry.

6. True or False: Janie loved her new freedom.
    A. True
    B. False

Multiple Choice Study Guide/Quiz Questions *Their Eyes Were Watching God*

Chapters 7-11 continued

7. What did Janie say about mourning and grief?
   A. She said they should both last for the same amount of time as one had known the person.
   B. She said they should not be expressed publicly.
   C. She said she mourned for Joe but grieved for herself.
   D. She said mourning shouldn't last any longer than grief.

8. How did Janie meet Tea Cake?
   A. Hezekiah introduced them.
   B. He came into the store and started talking to her.
   C. He was Phoeby's brother who was visiting, and she met him at church.
   D. She met him when she went into Orlando to do some shopping.

9. Which of the following does **not** describe Tea Cake?
   A. He had a full beard and mustache.
   B. He was tall.
   C. He was lean.
   D. He had full, lazy eyes.

10. Which of the following is **not** one of the main concerns that Janie had about getting into a relationship with Tea Cake?
    A. He was about twelve years younger than she was.
    B. He didn't look like he had much money.
    C. She wasn't sure his intentions were serious or honorable.
    D. She had not been a widow long enough to start another relationship.

11. True or False: Tea Cake visited Janie early one morning because he wanted to prove to her that he was not lazy.
    A. True
    B. False

12. What did Tea Cake do that proved his serious intentions toward Janie?
    A. He bought her a ring.
    B. He invited her to the big Sunday School picnic.
    C. He moved into town.
    D. He introduced her to his friends.

Multiple Choice Study Guide/Quiz Questions *Their Eyes Were Watching God*

Chapters 12-15

1. True or False: The townspeople were glad Janie was going out with Tea Cake. They liked seeing her happy.
    A. True
    B. False

2. What was Janie's response when Phoeby talked to her about Tea Cake?
    A. She said she was just having a fling for fun, but she was not serious about him.
    B. She got angry and told Phoeby to mind her own business.
    C. She said she had always wanted to go and do the things that she was doing with Tea Cake, but that Joe wouldn't let her.
    D. She said she thought a little bit of attention was good for business in the store.

3. Why did Janie want to sell the store?
    A. She didn't want people comparing Tea Cake to Joe if they were in the store.
    B. She wanted to use the money to go on a long honeymoon.
    C. She didn't want to be tied down to it for the rest of her life.
    D. The store had been losing money and she wanted to get out before it was too late.

4. Which of the following statements describes Janie and Tea Cake's wedding?
    A. They had a huge wedding in Eatonville, and invited everyone in the town.
    B. They had a quiet wedding with only Phoeby and Hezekiah present.
    C. They got married in Orlando, and after a few weeks, came back to Eatonville and had a reception at Janie's house.
    D. Tea Cake met Janie at the train station in Jacksonville and took her to the preacher's house, where they got married.

5. What did Janie discover one morning about a week after she was married?
    A. She woke up and discovered that Tea Cake had taken her $200 and gone out.
    B. She discovered that Tea Cake slept with a gun under his pillow.
    C. She found a list of his female friends in one of his shirt pockets.
    D. She found a bankbook and discovered that he was wealthy.

6. What did Janie tell Tea Cake after the above incident?
    A. She told him she wanted to go back home without him.
    B. She told him she expected him to share everything he had with her equally.
    C. She told him she was disappointed that he had not taken her into his confidence.
    D. She told him she intended to partake of everything with him, and if he ever went off and had fun without her again, she would kill him.

Multiple Choice Study Guide/Quiz Questions *Their Eyes Were Watching God*

Chapters 12-15 continued

7. How did Tea Cake get the money back?
    A. He went to work as a laborer.
    B. He robbed two stores.
    C. He gambled and won $322.00.
    D. He sold his clothes and his guitar.

8. Where did Janie and Tea Cake go, and why?
    A. They went to Orlando so Tea Cake could gamble.
    B. They went to the swamps to kill alligators and sell their skin.
    C. They went to Palm Beach to live a life of luxury with Janie's money.
    D. They went to the Everglades to pick beans.

9. Which of the following does **not** describe the muck?
    A. It was a section of the Everglades near Clewiston and Belle Glade.
    B. It was on a Seminole Indian reservation.
    C. Sugar cane, beans, and tomatoes grew there.
    D. It was near Lake Okechobee.

10. True or False: Janie enjoyed the work and the social life with Tea Cake.
    A. True
    B. False

11. Why did Janie start to go out and pick beans?
    A. They needed the money.
    B. She didn't trust Tea Cake among all of the other women.
    C. Tea Cake asked her to because he was lonely without her.
    D. The foreman said she had to or she couldn't live in the company house anymore.

12. What happened as a result of the incident with Nunkie?
    A. Janie beat up Nunkie and drove her out of the area.
    B. Tea Cake reassured Janie that she was the only woman in whom he was interested.
    C. Janie took up with another man for spite.
    D. Janie refused to go to work anymore.

Multiple Choice Study Guide/Quiz Questions *Their Eyes Were Watching God*

Chapters 16-18

1. Which of the following statements does **not** describe Mrs. Turner and her attitude about Negroes?
    A. Mrs. Turner was light-skinned, with Caucasian features.
    B. She was the product of a mixed marriage, and didn't really fit in either white or Negro society.
    C. She prided herself on not looking like the other Negroes.
    D. She did not like black Negroes, and thought herself better than them.

2. True or False: Mrs. Turner thought Janie was too fine-featured to be married to a man as black as Tea Cake. She wanted to introduce Janie to her brother.
    A. True
    B. False

3. What did Tea Cake do after Mrs. Turner introduced her brother to Janie and Tea Cake?
    A. He ran Mrs. Turner's brother out of town with a shotgun.
    B. He threatened to kill Mrs. Turner if she ever got near Janie again.
    C. He started locking Janie in the house when he went out.
    D. He whipped Janie to show that he was still in possession of her.

4. How did the men react to Tea Cake's treatment of Janie?
    A. They approved.
    B. They disapproved.

5. Which of the following did **not** happen during the incident in Mrs. Turner's restaurant?
    A. The place was full, so Coodemay tried to shove Sop-de-Bottom out of his chair.
    B. Tea Cake tried to take Coodemay and Serrent out of the restaurant, which started a general melee.
    C. Mrs. Turner was accidentally shot during the fight.
    D. The inside of the restaurant was in a shambles by the time the fight was over.

6. What was Mrs. Turner's reaction to the incident?
    A. She tried to sue all of the men who were in the restaurant.
    B. She told her husband she wanted to move back to Miami.
    C. She hired someone to kill Tea Cake.
    D. she was glad, because she collected a lot of insurance money for the damages.

Multiple Choice Study Guide/Quiz Questions *Their Eyes Were Watching God*

Chapters 16-18 continued

7. How did the people on the muck find out a hurricane was coming?
    A. The read about it in the newspaper.
    B. They heard it on the radio.
    C. One of the women in their group went into a trance and predicted it.
    D. They saw the Seminoles and the animals moving eastward.

8. Why did some of the people, including Tea Cake and Janie, remain in their houses on the muck?
    A. They didn't have enough money to leave.
    B. The boss had said that anyone who left would be fired. They didn't want to lose their jobs.
    C. They thought they were safe because of the dike.
    D. They had never seen a hurricane, and didn't understand how devastating one could be.

9. What was Janie's response when Tea Cake asked Janie if she wished she had stayed in her big house, away from dangers such as the hurricane?
    A. She said it was too late to think about those things.
    B. She said she didn't think she would die until her time came, and that she was happy being with Tea Cake.
    C. She said she was looking forward to the adventure.
    D. She said yes, she wished she had, and that she would go back home after the hurricane.

10. True or False: When the author used the sentence "They seemed to be staring at the dark, but their eyes were watching God," the people were in church during a candle-light service.
    A. True
    B. False

11. What did Janie and Teacake do to try and escape from the lake?
    A. They started swimming and walking toward the high road that went to Palm Beach.
    B. They borrowed a car.
    C. They stole a rowboat .
    D. They stayed on the roof of a house to wait out the storm.

12. True or False: The dog bit Tea Cake before he was able to kill it.
    A. True
    B. False

Multiple Choice Study Guide/Quiz Questions *Their Eyes Were Watching God*

Chapters 19-20

1. What did Janie and Tea Cake do after the hurricane was over?
    A. They stayed in Palm Beach.
    B. They went to Orlando.
    C. They went to Jacksonville.
    D. They went back to the muck.

2. What happened in the middle of their fourth week back on the muck?
    A. Tea Cake was injured on the job.
    B. Tea Cake was attacked by a swarm of bees.
    C. Tea Cake came home complaining of a headache.
    D. They found out their water was contaminated.

3. Which of the following was **not** one of Tea Cake's symptoms?
    A. He had a fever.
    B. He couldn't swallow.
    C. He had a rash all over.
    D. He became delirious.

4. True or False: The doctor told Janie that Tea Cake had yellow fever, and would probably recover in a week to ten days.
    A. True
    B. False

5. What did Janie do after the doctor left?
    A. She went outside and looked up at the sky. She wondered if God was noticing what was going on, and if he had intentionally caused this problem for her and Tea Cake.
    B. She asked the doctor find a good hospital for Tea Cake. She said she had plenty of money to pay for the best care possible.
    C. She wrote a letter to Phoeby and asked her to come and help her take Tea Cake home.
    D. She went to see the minister and asked him why bad things had to happen to good people.

6. What did Janie find under Tea Cake's pillow?
    A. She found his hunting knife.
    B. She found a love letter to her.
    C. She found the pills he was supposed to have taken earlier.
    D. She found his pistol, with three full chambers.

Multiple Choice Study Guide/Quiz Questions *Their Eyes Were Watching God*

Chapters 19-20 continued

7. What did Janie do after she found this?
    A. She readied the rifle and put it in a corner of the kitchen.
    B. She went outside and cried.
    C. She took it and hid it.
    D. She ran to the next house for help.

8. What happened when Tea Cake came back into the house?
    A. He went to bed and fell asleep.
    B. Janie and Tea Cake shot at the same time, and Janie shot and killed Tea Cake.
    C. He shot himself.
    D. He ran after Janie with his knife, tripped, and stabbed himself through the heart.

9. What happened just before Tea Cake died?
    A. Tea Cake bit Janie on the arm.
    B. Tea Cake regained his senses and told her he loved her.
    C. He tried to strangle Janie.
    D. Janie tried to shoot herself, but the pistol was empty.

10. What was the outcome of the trial?
    A. Janie was accused of murder and sent to prison.
    B. She was acquitted.

11. True or False: The other men from the muck who watched the trial wanted to testify in Janie's behalf.
    A. True
    B. False

12. What did Janie bring back to Eatonville?
    A. She brought back Tea Cake's pistol.
    B. She brought back Tea Cake's guitar.
    C. She brought back a jar of the muck.
    D. She brought the pack of seed that Tea Cake had wanted to plant.

ANSWER KEY MULTIPLE CHOICE STUDY GUIDE/QUIZ QUESTIONS
Their Eyes Were Watching God

Chapters 1-4	Chapters 5 & 6	Chapters 7-11
1. B False	1. D	1. A
2. B	2. B	2. B False
3. C	3. A	3. C
4. B	4. B False	4. C
5. A True	5. C	5. D
6. D	6. A	6. A True
7. A True	7. D	7. D
8. C	8. B	8. B
9. B False	9. A True	9. A
10. D	10. D	10. D
11. C	11. C	11. B False
12. A	12. A True	12. B

Chapters 12-15	Chapters 16-18	Chapters 19 & 20
1. B False	1. B	1. D
2. C	2. A True	2. C
3. A	3. D	3. C
4. D	4. A	4. B False
5. A	5. C	5. A
6. D	6. B	6. D
7. C	7. D	7. A
8. D	8. C	8. B
9. B	9. B	9. A
10. A True	10. B False	10. B
11. C	11. A	11. B False
12. B	12. A True	12. D

PREREADING VOCABULARY WORKSHEETS

PREREADING VOCABULARY WORKSHEETS *Their Eyes Were Watching God*

<u>Chapters 1-4</u>
Part I: Using Prior Knowledge and Context Clues
Below are the sentences in which the vocabulary words appear in the text. Read the sentence. Use any clues you can find in the sentence combined with your prior knowledge, and write what you think the underlined words mean on the lines provided.

1. For others they sail forever on the horizon, never out of sight, never landing until the Watcher turns his eyes away in *resignation*, his dreams mocked to death by Time.

   _____

2. She had come back from the *sodden* and the bloated; the sudden dead, their eyes flung wide open in judgment.

   _____

3. An envious heart makes a *treacherous* ear.

   _____

4. Then Janie felt a pain remorseless sweet that left her limp and *languid*.

   _____

5. The vision of Logan Killicks was *desecrating* the pear tree, but Janie didn't know how to tell Nanny that.

   _____

6. She bolted upright and peered out of the window and saw Johnny Taylor *lacerating* her Janie with a kiss.

   _____

7. She would *expound* what Ah felt.

   _____

Prereading Vocabulary Worksheets *Their Eyes Were Watching God*

8. Finally out of Nanny's talk and her own *conjectures* she made a sort of comfort for herself.

_____

9. He says he never mean to lay de weight uh his hand on me in *malice*.

_____

10. Nanny sent Janie along with a stern *mien*, but she dwindled all the rest of the day as she worked

_____

Part II: Determining the Meaning   Match the vocabulary words to their dictionary definitions.

1. resignation   A. Explain; give a detailed account
2. sodden   B. Manner or appearance
3. treacherous   C. Unresisting acceptance
4. languid   D. Not trustworthy; dangerous
5. desecrating   E. Thoroughly soaked; saturated
6. lacerating   F. Ideas formed from guessing
7. expound   G. Extreme ill will or spite
8. conjectures   H. Violating the sacredness of
9. malice   I. Lacking energy or vitality; weak
10. mien   J. Ripping, cutting, or tearing

Prereading Vocabulary Worksheets *Their Eyes Were Watching God*

Chapters 5-6
Part I: Using Prior Knowledge and Context Clues
Below are the sentences in which the vocabulary words appear in the text. Read the sentence. Use any clues you can find in the sentence combined with your prior knowledge, and write what you think the underlined words mean on the lines provided.

1. Guv'nor Amos Hicks from Buford, South Carolina. Free, single, *disengaged*.

_____

2. They got up and *sauntered* over to where Starks was living for the present.

_____

3. They tried hard to hold it in, but enough *incredulous* laughter burst out of their eyes and leaked from the corners of their mouths to inform anyone of their thoughts.

_____

4. Youse way outa *jurisdiction*.

_____

5. There was something about Joe Starks that *cowed* the town.

_____

6. He was next to the Mayor in *prominence*, and made better talking.

_____

7. They mocked everything human in death. Starks led off with a great *eulogy* on our departed citizen, our most distinguished citizen and the grief he left behind him. . . .

_____

Prereading Vocabulary Worksheets *Their Eyes Were Watching God*

8. Joe returned to the store full of pleasure and good humor but he didn't want Janie to notice it because he saw that she was *sullen* and he resented that.

_____

9. He wanted her *submission* and he'd keep on fighting until he felt he had it.

_____

10. He was *baiting* Mrs. Tony Robbins as he always did when she came to the store.

_____

Part II: Determining the Meaning   Match the vocabulary words to their dictionary definitions.

1. disengaged   A. Speech or praise about a dead person
2. sauntered   B. Taunting; teasing; luring
3. incredulous   C. Bullied
4. jurisdiction   D. Released, detached
5. cowed   E. The act of giving in to another
6. prominence   F. Strolled
7. eulogy   G. Area of control
8. sullen   H. Unbelieving, skeptical
9. submission   I. Morose or sulky
10. baiting   J. Widely known or easily identified

Prereading Vocabulary Worksheets *Their Eyes Were Watching God*

Chapters 7-11
Part I: Using Prior Knowledge and Context Clues
Below are the sentences in which the vocabulary words appear in the text. Read the sentence. Use any clues you can find in the sentence combined with your prior knowledge, and write what you think the underlined words mean on the lines provided.

1. Then one day she sat and watched the shadow of herself going about tending store and *prostrating* itself before Jody, while all the time she herself sat under a shady tree. . . .

_____

2. His prosperous-looking belly that used to thrust out so *pugnaciously* and intimidate folks, sagged like a load suspended from his loins.

_____

3. They came to the store and *ostentatiously* looked over whatever she was doing and went back to report to him at the house.

_____

4. A sound of strife in Jody's throat, but his eyes stared unwillingly into a corner of the room so Janie knew the *futile* fight was not with her.

_____

5. Then again the gold and red and purple, the gloat and glamour of the secret orders, each with its *insinuations* of power and glory undreamed of by the uninitiated.

_____

6. She almost apologized to the tenants the first time she collected the rents. Felt like a *usurper*.

_____

7. You spoke of honor and respect. And all that they said and did was *refracted* by her inattention and shot off towards the rim-bones of nothing.

_____

Prereading Vocabulary Worksheets *Their Eyes Were Watching God*

8. He struggled *gallantly* to free himself.

_____

9. "Ah just had one," Jane *temporized* with her conscience.

_____

10. This was a new sensation for her, but no less *excruciating*.

_____

Part II: Determining the Meaning Match the vocabulary words to their dictionary definitions.

1. prostrating
2. pugnaciously
3. ostentatiously
4. futile
5. insinuations
6. usurper
7. refracted
8. gallantly
9. temporized
10. excruciating

A. Negotiated to gain time
B. Having no useful result
C. Intensely painful; agonizing
D. Boldly; nobly
E. Bowing in adoration or submission
F. Light deflected from a straight path
G. Combative in nature; belligerent
H. In a pompous manner or showing off
I. Subtly made suggestions
J. One who grabs property or money

Prereading Vocabulary Worksheets *Their Eyes Were Watching God*

Chapters 12-15
Part I: Using Prior Knowledge and Context Clues
Below are the sentences in which the vocabulary words appear in the text. Read the sentence. Use any clues you can find in the sentence combined with your prior knowledge, and write what you think the underlined words mean on the lines provided.

1. Janie acted glad to see her and after a while Phoeby *broached* her with, "Janie, everybody's talkin' 'bout how dat Tea Cake is draggin' you round tuh places you ain't used tuh."

_____

2. Ah'd feel uh whole heap better 'bout yuh if you wuz marryin' dat man up dere in Sanford. He got somethin' tuh put long side uh whut you got and dat make it more better. He's *endurable*.

_____

3. So Ah got up on de high stool lak she told me, but Pheoby, Ah done nearly *languished* tuh death up dere.

_____

4. The room inside looked like the mouth of an alligator--*gaped* wide open to swallow something down.

_____

5. She got out of the bed but a chair couldn't hold her. She *dwindled* down on the floor with her head in a rocking chair.

_____

6. Let the old *hypocrites* learn to mind their own business, and leave other folks alone.

_____

7. Permanent *transients* with no attachments and tired looking men with their families and dogs in flivvers.

_____

Prereading Vocabulary Worksheets *Their Eyes Were Watching God*

8. Tea Cake didn't seem to be able to *fend* her off as promptly as Janie thought he ought to.

___

9. Then when her ready cash was gone, had come Who Flung to denounce his *predecessor* as a scoundrel and took up all around the house himself.

___

10. Shining their *phosphorescent* eyes and shooting them in the dark.

___

Part II: Determining the Meaning   Match the vocabulary words to their dictionary definitions.

1. broached   A. Brought up for discussion
2. endurable   B. People who say one thing but do the opposite
3. languished   C. Resist; push away; shield
4. gaped   D. Long-lasting; able to be tolerated for a long time
5. dwindled   E. Travelers without permanent homes
6. hypocrites   F. Wasted away; weakened
7. transients   G. Became gradually smaller until little or nothing remained
8. fend   H. Held open as if yawning
9. predecessor   I. Emission of light without burning
10. phosphorescent   J. An ancestor; a forebearer

Prereading Vocabulary Worksheets *Their Eyes Were Watching God*

Chapters 16-18
Part I: Using Prior Knowledge and Context Clues
Below are the sentences in which the vocabulary words appear in the text. Read the sentence. Use any clues you can find in the sentence combined with your prior knowledge, and write what you think the underlined words mean on the lines provided.

1. For instance during the summer when she heard the *subtle* but compelling rhythms of the Bahaman drummers, she's walk over and watch the dances.

   _____

2. According to all Janie had been taught this was *sacrilege* so she sat without speaking at all.

   _____

3. It was *inevitable* that she should accept any inconsistency and cruelty from her deity as all good worshipers do from theirs.

   _____

4. Two or three people who were not there during the *fracas* poked their heads in at the door to sympathize but that made Mrs. Turner madder.

   _____

5. The men walking in front and the laden, *stolid* women following them like burros.

   _____

6. It was hot and *sultry* and Janie left the field and went home.

   _____

7. Through the screaming wind they heard things crashing and things hurtling and dashing with unbelievable *velocity*.

   _____

Prereading Vocabulary Worksheets *Their Eyes Were Watching God*

8. Ten feet higher and as far as they could see the muttering wall advanced before the braced-up waters like a road crusher on a *cosmic* scale.

___

9. He saw a cow swimming slowly towards the fill in an *oblique* line.

___

10. A great deal of *perseverance* and they found a place to sleep.

___

Part II: Determining the Meaning   Match the vocabulary words to their dictionary definitions.

1. subtle   A. Having or showing little emotion
2. sacrilege   B. Speed
3. inevitable   C. Against something sacred
4. fracas   D. A fight; a brawl
5. stolid   E. Persistence; dogged trying
6. sultry   F. Very hot and humid
7. velocity   G. Universal; vast
8. cosmic   H. Quiet; difficult to detect
9. oblique   I. Slanted
10. perseverance   J. Unavoidable

Prereading Vocabulary Worksheets *Their Eyes Were Watching God*

Chapters 19-20
Part I: Using Prior Knowledge and Context Clues
Below are the sentences in which the vocabulary words appear in the text. Read the sentence. Use any clues you can find in the sentence combined with your prior knowledge, and write what you think the underlined words mean on the lines provided.

1. Dis town is full uh trouble and *compellment*.

   _____

2. So de white man figger dat anything less than de Uncle Sam's *consolidated* water closet would be too easy.

   _____

3. Tea Cake took it and filled his mouth then gagged horribly, *disgorged* that which was in his mouth and threw the glass upon the floor.

   _____

4. He slapped Tea Cake *lustily* across his back and Tea Cake tried to smile as he was expected to do.

   _____

5. Her arms went up in a desperate *supplication* for a minute.

   _____

6. He gave her a look full of blank *ferocity* and gurgled in his throat.

   _____

7. She noted that even in his *delirium* he took good aim.

   _____

Prereading Vocabulary Worksheets *Their Eyes Were Watching God*

8. The *fiend* in him must kill and Janie was the only thing living he saw.

___

9. The wind through the open windows had broomed out all the *fetid* feeling of absence and nothingness.

___

10. If you find her a *wanton* killer you must bring in a verdict of first degree murder.

___

Part II: Determining the Meaning   Match the vocabluary words to their dictionary definitions.

1. compellment
2. consolidated
3. disgorged
4. lustily
5. supplication
6. ferocity
7. delirium
8. fiend
9. fetid
10. wanton

A. Mental confusion caused by illness
B. Plea; earnest request
C. Strong forces
D. Having an offensive odor
E. Vomited; threw up
F. Bad or evil person
G. Savageness; fierceness
H. Robustly; strongly
I. Cruel; merciless
J. United into one system; combined

ANSWER KEY
Prereading Vocabulary Worksheets *Their Eyes Were Watching God*

Chapters 1-4
1. C
2. E
3. D
4. I
5. H
6. J.
7. A
8. F
9. G
10. B

Chapters 5-6
1. D
2. F
3. H
4. G
5. C
6. J
7. A
8. I
9. E
10. B

Chapters 7-11
1. E
2. G
3. H
4. B
5. I
6. J
7. F
8. D
9. A
10. C

Chapters 12-15
1. A
2. D
3. F
4. H
5. G
6. B
7. E
8. C
9. J
10. I

Chapters 16-18
1. H
2. C
3. J
4. D
5. A
6. F
7. B
8. G
9. I
10. E

Chapters 19-20
1. C
2. J
3. E
4. H
5. B
6. G
7. A
8. F
9. D
10. I

DAILY LESSON PLANS

LESSON ONE

Objectives
    1. To introduce the *Their Eyes Were Watching God* unit
    2. To relate students' prior knowledge to the new material
    3. To distribute books and other related materials (study guides, reading assignments)
    4. To introduce the use of dialect
    5. To do the prereading work for Chapters 1-4

Activity #1
    Show some pictures of rural Florida in the 1930s. If possible, show pictures of an all-black town in the South. Ask students to tell you what they know about Florida in general, about Zora Neale Hurston, and about the novel. Do a group KWL sheet with the students (form included.) Put any information the students know in the K column (What I Know.) Ask students what they want to find out and put that information in the W column (What I Want to Find Out.) Keep the sheet and refer back to it while reading. After reading the novel, complete the L column (What I Learned.)

Activity #2
    Distribute the materials students will use in this unit. Explain in detail how students are to use these materials.

    Study Guides Students should preview the study guide questions before each reading assignment to get a feeling for what events and ideas are important in that section. After reading the section, students will (as a class or individually) answer the questions to review the important events and ideas from that section of the book. Students should keep the study guides as study materials for the unit test.

    Reading Assignment Sheet You need to fill in the reading assignment sheet to let students know when their reading has to be completed. You can either write the assignment sheet on a side blackboard or bulletin board and leave it there for students to see each day, or you can make copies for each student to have. In either case, you should advise students to become very familiar with the reading assignments so they know what is expected of them.

    Extra Activities Center The resource materials portion of this unit contains suggestions for a library of related books and articles in your classroom as well as crossword and word search puzzles. Make an extra activities center in your room where you will keep these materials for students to use. (Bring the books and articles in from the library and keep several copies of the puzzles on hand.) Explain to students that these materials are available for students to use when they finish reading assignments or other class work early.

    Books Each school has its own rules and regulations regarding student use of school books. Advise students of the procedures that are normal for your school.

Activity #3

Introduce the use of Southern Black dialect in the novel. There is an audio tape version of the novel available. This would be a good time to play part of it, so students can hear the dialect. Otherwise, find another movie or audio cassette that uses dialect and play it. You may want to make a list of words spoken in dialect and their formal English equivalent.

Activity #4

Show students how to preview the study questions and do the vocabulary work for Chapters 1-4 of *Their Eyes Were Watching God*. If students do not finish this assignment in class, they should complete it prior to the next class meeting.

LESSON ONE *Their Eyes Were Watching God*

KWL *Their Eyes Were Watching God*

Directions: Before reading, think about what you already know about Zora Neale Hurston and/or *Their Eyes Were Watching God* Write the information in the K column. Think about what you would like to find out from reading the book. Write your questions in the W column. After you have read the book, use the L column to write the answers to your questions from the W column, and anything else you remember from the book.

K	**W**	**L**
What I Know	**What I Want to Find Out**	**What I Learned**

LESSON TWO

Objectives
1. To read Chapters 1-4
2. To review the main ideas and events from Chapters 1-4
3. To introduce the Nonfiction assignment

Activity #1

You may want to read Chapter 1 aloud to the students to set the mood for the novel. Invite willing students to read Chapters 2-4 aloud to the rest of the class. Students with some acitng ability may enjoy the challenge of reading aloud using the dialect.

Activity #2

Give the students time to answer the study guide questions, and then discuss the answers in detail. Write the answers on the board or overhead projector so students can have the correct answers for study purposes. Encourage students to take notes. If the students own their books, encourage them to use highlighter pens to mark important passages and the answers to the study guide questions.

Note: It is a good practice in public speaking and leadership skills for individuals students to take charge of leading the discussion of the study questions. Perhaps a different student could go to the front of the class and lead the discussion each day that the study questions are discussed during this unit. Of course, the teacher should guide the discussion when appropriate and be sure to fill in any gaps the students leave.

Activity #3

Distribute copies of the Nonfiction Assignment sheet and go over it in detail with the students. Give them the due date for the assignment (Lesson 17.)

NONFICTION ASSIGNMENT SHEET *Their Eyes Were Watching God*

(To be completed after reading the required nonfiction article)

Name _____ Date _____ Class _____

Title of Nonfiction Read _____

Written By _____ Publication Date _____

I. Factual Summary: Write a short summary of the piece you read.

II. Vocabulary:
    1. With which vocabulary words in the piece did you encounter some degree of difficulty?

    2. How did you resolve your lack of understanding with these words?

III. Interpretation: What was the main point the author wanted you to get from reading his/her work?

IV. Criticism:
    1. With which points of the piece did you agree or find easy to accept? Why?

    2. With which points of the piece did you disagree or find difficult to believe? Why?

V. Personal Response: What do you think about this piece? OR How does this piece influence your ideas?

LESSON THREE

Objectives
    1. To do the prereading and vocabulary work for chapters 5-6
    2. To read Chapters 5-6
    3. To give students practice reading orally
    4. To evaluate students' oral reading

Activity #1

    Give students about fifteen minutes to preview the study questions for Chapters 5-6 and do the related vocabulary work.

Activity #2

    Have students read chapters 5-6 of *Their Eyes Were Watching God* out loud in class. You probably know the best way to get readers with your class; pick students at random, ask for volunteers, or use whatever method works best for your group. Since much of the book is written in dialog, you may want to have different students read the parts of the characters, and also the narrator. If you have not yet completed an oral reading evaluation for your students for this marking period, this would be a good opportunity to do so. A form is included with this unit for your convenience.

    If students do not complete reading Chapters 5-6 in class, they should do so prior to your next class meeting.

LESSON FOUR

Objectives
    1. To check students' understanding of the main ideas and events from Chapters 5-6
    2. To preview the study questions and vocabulary for Chapters 7-11
    3. To read Chapters 7-11

Activity #1

    Quiz--distribute quizzes (multiple choice study questions for Chapters 1-6) and give students about ten minutes to complete them. Have students exchange papers. Grade the quizzes as a class. Collect the papers for recording the grades.

Activity #2

    Give students about fifteen minutes to preview the study questions for Chapters 7-11 and do the related vocabulary work.

Activity #3

    Have students read Chapters 7-11 for the rest of the period. If you have not completed the oral reading evaluations, do so now. If the evaluations have been completed, you may want the students to read silently. If students do not complete the reading assignment in class, they should do so prior to your next class meeting.

ORAL READING EVALUATION *Their Eyes Were Watching God*

Name_____Class_____Date_____--

SKILL	EXCELLENT	GOOD	AVERAGE	FAIR	POOR
Fluency	5	4	3	2	1
Clarity	5	4	3	2	1
Audibility	5	4	3	2	1
Pronunciation	5	4	3	2	1
_____	5	4	3	2	1
_____	5	4	3	2	1

Total _____ Grade _____

Comments:

LESSON FIVE

Objectives
1. To give students the opportunity to practice writing a public service announcement
2. To give the teacher the opportunity to evaluate each student's writing skills

Activity #1

Distribute Writing Assignment #1 and discuss the directions in detail. Allow the remaining class time for students to work on the assignment. Give students an additional two or three days to complete the assignment, if necessary.

Activity #2

Distribute copies of the Writing Evaluation Form (included in this Unit Plan.) Explain to students that during Lesson Nine you will be holding individual writing conferences about this writing assignment. Make sure they are familiar with the criteria on the Writing Evaluation Form.

Follow-Up: After you have graded the assignments, have a writing conference with each student, (This unit schedules one in Lesson Nine.) After the writing conference, allow students to revise their papers using your suggestions to complete the revision. I suggest grading the revisions on an A-C-E scale (all revisions well-done, some revisions made, few or no revisions made.) This will speed your grading time and still give some credit for the students' efforts.

LESSON SIX

Objectives
1. To review the main ideas and events in Chapters 7-11
2. To preview the study questions and vocabulary for Chapters 12-15
3. To read Chapters 12-15 silently

Activity #1

Ask students to get out their books and some paper (not their study guides.) Tell student to write down ten questions and answers which cover the main events and ideas in Chapters 7-11. Discuss the students' questions and answers orally, making a list on the board of the questions with brief responses. Put a star next to students' questions and answers that are essentially the same and the study guide questions. Be sure that all of the study guide questions are answered.

Activity #2

Give students about fifteen minutes to do the prereading and vocabulary work for Chapters 12-15.

Activity #3

Give students the remainder of the period to begin silently reading Chapters 12-15. Remind them that the reading must be completed prior to your next class meeting.

WRITING ASSIGNMENT 1 *Their Eyes Were Watching God*

PROMPT

Later on in the story you will read about a hurricane that takes place in Florida.

Your assignment is to write a public service announcement for television or radio. It should explain what a hurricane is, and what to do in the event that you are caught in one.

PREWRITING

The first thing you need to do is decide whether you want to do television or radio. Radio has no visual input, so your explanation and directions must be very clear and easy to understand. A televison announcement would need several visuals in the form of posters, charts, or photographs. In order to be accurate, you will also have to do some research on hurricanes. Your school or public library will have books, encyclopedias, newspaper articles, and possibly videos having to do with hurricanes.

DRAFTING

First, write a paragraph in which you explain what a hurricane is. Tell about the speed of the winds, the amount of rain that can be expected,.how long the storm may last, and the kind of damage tjhat is possible. You may want to talk about a recent hurricane as an eaxample.

In the body of your paper, explain what to do in case of a hurricane. You may find it easier to use a list format here instead of a paragraph. Give information on when to evacuate, where to go, what to bring with you. Include phone numbers for relief groups such as the Red Cross. If you are doing the television version, have charts, tables, and pictures available.

Finally, write a concluding paragraph that tells again what a hurricane is, and why your listeners should obey the advice given by the professionals.

PROMPT

When you finish the rough draft of your paper, ask another student to read it. After reading your rough draft, he/she should tell you what he/she liked best about your work, which parts were difficult to understand, and ways in which your work could be improved. Reread your paper considering your critic's comments, and make the corrections you think are necessary.

PROOFREADING

Do a final proofreading of your paper, double-checking your grammar, spelling, organization, and the clarity of your ideas.

WRITING EVALUATION FORM *Their Eyes Were Watching God*

Name _____ Date _____ Class _____

Writing Assignment #1 for *Their Eyes Were Watching God*

Circle One For Each Item:

Introduction	excellent	good	fair	poor
Body Paragraphs	excellent	good	fair	poor
Summary	excellent	good	fair	poor
Grammar	excellent	good	fair	poor (errors noted)
Spelling	excellent	good	fair	poor (errors noted)
Punctuation	excellent	good	fair	poor (errors noted)
Legibility	excellent	good	fair	poor (errors noted)

Strengths:

Weaknesses:

Comments/Suggestions:

LESSON SEVEN

Objectives
>   1. To review the main ideas and events from Chapters 12-15
>   2. To preview the study questions and vocabulary for Chapters 16-18
>   3. To read Chapters 16-18

Activity #1
>   Review the study guide questions and answers for Chapters 12-15

Activity #2
>   Give students about fifteen minutes to complete the prereading and vocabulary work for Chapters 16-18.

Activity #3
>   Depending on the needs of your group, have the students read these chapters orally or silently. Remind them that any reading not completed in class must be finished before the next class meeting.

LESSON EIGHT

Objectives
>   1. To check to see that students have done the required reading
>   2. To introduce Writing Assignment #2

Activity #1
>   Give students a quiz on Chapters 16-18. Use either the short answer or multiple choice form of the study guide questions as a quiz so that in discussing the answers to the quiz you also answer the study guide questions. Collect the papers for grading.

Activity #2
>   Distribute Writing Assignment #2. Discuss the directions in detail and give students ample time to complete the assignment.

LESSON NINE

<u>Objectives</u>
1. To have students revise their first writing assignment papers
2. To work on other assignments independently

<u>Activity #1</u>
Call students to your desk or some other private area to discuss their papers from Writing Assignment #1. Use the completed Writing Evaluation Form as a basis for your critique.

<u>Activity #2</u>
Students should use this period (when they are not conferencing with you) work on their Nonfiction assignment, or to review the study guide questions they have covered so far.

WRITING ASSIGNMENT #2 *Their Eyes Were Watching God*

PROMPT

You are a sales representative for a large company. The town of Eatonville, Florida, is in your territory. You have heard that the general store in Eatonville does a high volume of business. You would like to have your products stocked on the shelves there. Your assignment is to make a sales presentation to the owner, Joe Starks.

PREWRITING

First, decide what kind of goods your company sells. It could be gourmet foods, toys, clothing, books, tools, etc. Then decide what kind of presentation you want to make-low key or high pressure. Think about using visual aids, such as sales charts, pictures of people using your products, testimonials from other businesses/consumers about the value of your product. A good salesperson gets to know his/her audience first, so make sure you reread the parts of the story that deal with Joe and the people of Eatonville so you know how to approach him.

DRAFTING

Begin with an introductory paragraph in which you introduce yourself and your company. Give a brief history of the company, as well as some professional information about yourself.

In the body of the sales presentation, explain the products in detail. Use your sales charts and other visuals to demonstrate the product's quality, and its current rate of sale. Use the background knowledge you have about the community and the store owner to make your "pitch" about why he should stock your products. Offer a percentage of the gross receipts and some kind of incentive bonus to Joe for the amount of your product that he sells each month.

In your summary, restate why it would be to Joe's benefit to stock your products.

PROMPT

When you finish the rough draft of your paper, ask a student who sits near you to read it. After reading your rough draft, he/she should tell you what he/she liked best about your work, which parts were difficult to understand, and ways in which your work could be improved. Reread your paper considering your critic's comments, and make the corrections you think are necessary.

PROOFREADING

Do a final proofreading of your paper double-checking your grammar, spelling, organization, and the clarity of your ideas.

LESSON TEN

Objectives
1. To complete the prereading and vocabulary work for Chapters 19-20
2. To silently read chapters 19-20
3. To review the main ideas and events from Chapters 19-20
4. To make sure the students have the answers to all of the previous study guide questions

Activity #1
Give students about fifteen minutes to preview the study questions and do the related vocabulary work.

Activity #2
Have students read the chapters silently and answer the study guide questions.

Activity #3
Go over the study guide questions for Chapters 19-20.

Activity #4
Give students time to go through their study guides and notes to see if they are missing any information. Let them work with partners to fill in the gaps, and be available for private consultations.

LESSON ELEVEN

Objective
To discuss *Their Eyes Were Watching God* at the interpretive and critical levels

Activity #1
Choose the questions from the Extra Writing Assignments/Discussion Questions which seem most appropriate for your students. A class discussion of these questions is most effective if students have been given the opportunity to formulate answers to the questions prior to the discussion. To this end, you may either have all the students formulate answers to all the questions, divide the class into groups and assign one or more questions to each group, or you could assign one questions to each student in your class. The option you choose will make a difference in the amount of class time needed for this activity.

Activity #2
After students have had ample time to formulate answers to the questions, begin your class discussion of the questions and the ideas presented by the questions. Be sure students take note during the discussion so they have information to study for the unit test.

EXTRA WRITING ASSIGNMENT/ DISCUSSION QUESTIONS
Their Eyes Were Watching God

Interpretive

1. From what point of view is the novel written? How does this affect your understanding of the story?
2. Discuss the main themes in the novel.
4. Discuss Janie's emergence as a person, and the roles that her three husbands had in her development.
5. Discuss the symbolism in the use of the horizon in the novel.
6. Discuss the symbolic importance of the mule and the "mule talk" in the novel.
7. Discuss the significance of the muck dweller's reaction to the oncoming hurricane and Hurston's sentence: "They seemed to be staring at the dark, but their eyes were watching God."
8. Which of the following placed the most limits on Janie: race, sex, class, or attitudes of others? Support your answer with examples from the novel.
9. What does Janie's reaction to Joe's criticism in Chapters 5 and 6 show about her character?
10. What did Joe's treatment of the mule show us about his personality?
11. What did Janie mean when she told Phoeby that Tea Cake had taught her "the maiden language all over again"?
12. Discuss Hurston's use of the pear tree as a symbol in the novel.
13. How did Janie's view of marriage change over the course of the novel? Use examples from the text to support your answer.

Critical

14. Which of Janie's husbands was best defined? Give examples from the novel.
15. During the trial, Hurston used the third person to summarize what Janie said. Would it have been more effective to have Janie speak at the trial in first person? Why or why not?
16. Was Hurston's portrayal of life in a Southern Black environment effective?
17. Some writers of the Harlem Renaissance felt that Hurston had not adequately portrayed the life of a Black woman. Others thought she had done an outstanding job. With which opinion do you agree? Why?
18. Was the use of free indirect discourse effective in the presentation of the novel?

Personal Response

19. How does the use of dialect affect your enjoyment of the novel?
20. Which of the characters did you like? Why?
21. Which of the characters did you dislike? Why?
22. Which scene in the story did you like most? Why?
23. Was the title effective? Why or why not?
24. What other title would have been appropriate for this book?
25. Would you recommend this book to a friend? Why or why not?

QUOTATIONS *Their Eyes Were Watching God*
Discuss the significance of the following quotations.

1. "So when we looked at de picture and everybody got pointed out there wasn't nobody left except a real dark little girl with long hair standing by Eleanort. Sat's where Ah wuz s'posed to be, but Ah couldn't recognize dat dark chile as me. So Ah ast, 'where is me? Ah don't see me.' "

2. "Naw. We been tuhgether round two years. If you kin see de light at daybreak, you don't keer if you die at dusk. It's so many people never see de light at all. Ah wuz fumblin' round and God opened de door."

3. "But nothing van't stop you from wishin'. You can't beat nobody down so low till you can rob 'em of they will.

4. "Somebody got to think for women and chillun and chickens and cows. I god, they sho don't think none theirselves."

5. "Naw, Ah needs two mules dis yeah. Taters is goin' tuh be taters in de fall. Bringin' in big prices. Ah aims tuh run two plows, and dis man Ah'm talkin' 'bout is got uh mule all gentled up so even uh woman kin handle 'im."

6. "Ah knowed you wans't goingtuh lissen tuh me. You changes everything but nothin' don't change you-not even death."

7. "Janie, Ah hope god may kill me, if Ah'm lyin'. Nobody else on earth kin hold uh candle tuh you, baby. You got de keys to de kingdom."

8. "Ah don't want yo' feathers always crumpled by folks throwin' up things in yo' face. And Ah can't die easy thinkin' maybe de menfolks white or black is makin' a spittin' cup outa you. Have some sympathy fuh me. Put me down easy, Janie, Ah'm a cracked plate."

9. "Thanky, Ma'am. But 'sposing you wuz tuh die, now. You wouldn't git mad at me for draggin' yuh heah?"

10. "Lawd! Ah done growed ten feet higher from jus' listenin' tuh you, Janie. Ah ain't satidfied wid mahself no mo'. "

11. " 'Cause you told me Ah mus gointer love him, and, Ah don't. Maybe if somebody was to tell me how, Ah could do it."

12. "Naw, Jody, it wasn't because Ah didn't have no sympathy. Ah had uh lavish uh dat. Ah just didn't never git no chance tuh use none of it. You wouldn't let me."

13. "She tore off the kerchief from her head and let down her plentiful hair. The weight, the length, the glory was there."

14. "If people thinks de same they can make it all right. So in the beginnin' new thoughts had tuh be thought and new words said. After Ah got used tuh dat, we gits 'long jus' fine. He done taught me de maiden language all over.'

15. "Naw. We been tuhgether round two years. If you kin see de light at daybreak, you don't keer if you die at dusk. It's so many people never see de light at all. Ah wuz fumblin' round and God opened de door."

LESSON TWELVE

<u>Objectives</u>
    1. To introduce Writing Assignment #3
    2. To give students time to work on the writing assignment

<u>Activity #1</u>
    Distribute copies of Writing Assignment #3. Discuss the directions in detail and give students ample time to complete the assignment.

LESSON THIRTEEN

<u>Objectives</u>
    1. To give students the opportunity to do research for their Nonfiction Assignment
    2. To assist students in the proper use of the school library

<u>Activity</u>
    Take your class to the library for the entire class period. Tell them they can have the time to work on their Nonfiction Assignment. Students who have completed the assignment can use the time to read for pleasure.

WRITING ASSIGNMENT # 3 *Their Eyes Were Watching God*

PROMPT
When Joe died, Phoeby told Janie she should marry again. Janie did marry Tea Cake. Now that Tea Cake has died and Janie has returned to Eatonville, she will have to make plans for her future. You are a new author who has decided to write a sequel to Their Eyes Were Watching God. You must submit your ideas to the editors at a publishing company and see if they will give you a contract to write the book. Your assignment is to outline what will happen next in Janie's life and write a sample first chapter. Your chapter only needs to be two or three pages long.

PREWRITING
The first thing you need to do is jot down ideas about what Janie could do and the conflicts she may have. Be creative! List all of your ideas. Then, go through them and highlight the three or four that you think would work together to make a good story. Put them in sequential order. Think about the characters from the first novel. Who will you keep? Which ones are not necessary to your plot? What new characters will you introduce? Also think about the setting. Will you have Janie stay in Eatonville? Will she go back to the muck? Perhaps she will travel to another city or state.

DRAFTING
First, develop the outline. You may want to make a graphic organizer. Make sure to include all of the information you thought about in the prewriting stage. If you are artistic, include a few drawings. Then, write the sample chapter.

PROMPT
After you have finished a rough draft of your outline and chapter, revise them until you are happy with your work. Then ask another student to tell you what he/she likes best about your work, and what things he/she thinks can be improved. Take another look at your work, keeping in mind your critic's suggestions, and make the revisions you feel are necessary.

PROOFREADING
Do a final proofreading of your paper double-checking your grammar, spelling, organization, and the clarity of your ideas.

LESSON FOURTEEN

Objective
    To review all of the vocabulary work done in this unit

VOCABULARY REVIEW ACTIVITIES

1. Divide your class into two teams and have an old-fashioned spelling or definition bee.

2. Give each of your students (or students in groups of two, three or four) a *Their Eyes Were Watching God* Vocabulary Word Search Puzzle. The person (group) to find all of the vocabulary words in the puzzle first wins.

3. Give students a *Their Eyes Were Watching God* Vocabulary Word Search Puzzle without the word list. The person or group to find the most vocabulary words in the puzzle wins.

4. Use a *Their Eyes Were Watching God* Vocabulary Crossword Puzzle. Put the puzzle onto a transparency on the overhead projector (so everyone can see it), and do the puzzle together as a class.

5. Give students a *Their Eyes Were Watching God* Vocabulary Matching Worksheet to do.

6. Divide your class into two teams. Use the *Their Eyes Were Watching God* vocabulary words with their letters jumbled as a word list. Student 1 from Team A faces off against Student 1 from Team B. You write the first jumbled word on the board. The first student (1A or 1B) to unscramble the word wins the chance for his/her team to score points. If 1A wins the jumble, go to student 2A and give him/her a definition. He/she must give you the correct spelling of the vocabulary word which fits that definition. If he/she does, Team A scores a point, and you give student 3A a definition for which you expect a correctly spelled matching vocabulary word. Continue giving Team A definitions until some team member makes an incorrect response. An incorrect response sends the game back to the jumbled-word face off, this time with students 2A and 2B. Instead of repeating giving definitions to the first few students of each team, continue with the student after the one who gave the last incorrect response on the team. For example, if Team B wins the jumbled-word face-off, and student 5B gave the last incorrect answer for Team B, you would start this round of definition questions with student 6B, and so on. The team with the most points wins!

7. Have students write a story in which they correctly use as many vocabulary words as possible. Have students read their compositions orally. Post the most original compositions on your bulletin board!

LESSON FIFTEEN

Objective
To study in more detail some of the main characters in *Their Eyes Were Watching God*

Activity #1
Divide your class into groups, one for each of the following:
1. Janie Mae Crawford
2. Nanny
3. Logan Killicks
4. Joe Starks
5. Tea Cake
6. Phoeby Watson
7. Mrs. Turner
8. Doctor Simmons

Each group should write down the characteristics of the character they are assigned. Then they should confer and form an opinion about that character.

Activity #2
Have a spokesperson from each group report the group's findings. Encourage the rest of the class to ask questions. If they disagree with the opinions of the reporting group, they must present evidence from the book to support their argument.

You may want to have a large piece of paper on the chalkboard or bulletin board. Put the name of each of the characters at the top of the chart. Have a writer from each group record the characteristics of the group. Students with artistic ability could draw their interpretations of what the characters look like.

LESSON SIXTEEN

Objectives
1. To watch a movie version of the novel *Their Eyes Were Watching God*
2. To compare and contrast the movie with the novel

Activity #1
The movie version of *Their Eyes Were Watching God* is available in many video stores, and through educational film distributors. Show the movie in class.

Activity #2
Discuss the ways in which the movie and the novel were similar and different. Discuss the reasons for the differences. You may want the students to write a short comparison/contrast paper after this discussion.

LESSON SEVENTEEN

<u>Objectives</u>

    1. To widen the breadth of students' knowledge about the topics discussed or touched upon in *Their Eyes Were Watching God*

    2. To check students' non-fiction assignments.

<u>Activity</u>

    Ask each student to give a brief oral report about the nonfiction work he/she read for the nonfiction assignment. Your criteria for evaluating this report will vary depending on the level of your students. You may wish for students to give a complete report without using notes of any kind, or you may want students to read directly from a written report, or you may want to do something in between these two extremes. Just make students aware of your criteria in ample time for them to prepare their reports.

    Start with one student's report, After that, ask if anyone else in the class has read on a topic related to the first student's report. If no one has, choose another student at random. After each report, be sure to ask if anyone has a report related to the one just completed. That will help keep a continuity during the discussion of the reports.

LESSON EIGHTEEN

Objective

    To review the main ideas presented in *Their Eyes Were Watching God*

Activity #1

    Choose one of the review games/activities included in the packet and spend your class period as outlined there.

Activity #2

    Remind students of the date for the Unit Test. Stress the review of the Study Guides and their class notes as a last minute, brush-up review for homework.

REVIEW GAMES / ACTIVITIES

1. Ask the class to make up a unit test for *Their Eyes Were Watching God*. The test should have 4 sections: multiple choice, true/false, short answer and essay. Students may use 1/2 period to make the test, including a separate answer sheet, and then swap papers and use the other 1/2 class period to take a test a classmate has devised. (open book)

2. Take 1/2 period for students to make up true and false questions (including the answers). Collect the papers and divide the class into two teams. Draw a big tic-tac-toe board on the chalk board. Make one team X and one team O. Ask questions to each side, giving each student one turn. If the question is answered correctly, that student's team's letter (X or O) is placed in the box. If the answer is incorrect, no mark is placed in the box. The object is to get three marks in a row like tic-tac-toe. You may want to keep track of the number of games won for each team.

3. Take 1/2 period for students to make up questions (true/false and short answer). Collect the questions. Divide the class into two teams. You'll alternate asking questions to individual members of teams A & B (like in a spelling bee). The question keeps going from A to B until it is correctly answered, then a new question is asked. A correct answer does not allow the team to get another question. Correct answers are +2 points; incorrect answers are -1 point.

4. Allow students time to quiz each other (in pairs) from their study guides and class notes.

5. Give students a *Their Eyes Were Watching God* crossword puzzle to complete.

6. Divide your class into two teams. Use the *Their Eyes Were Watching God* crossword words with their letters jumbled as a word list. Student 1 from Team A faces off against Student 1 from Team B. You write the first jumbled word on the board. The first student (1A or 1B) to unscramble the word wins the chance for his/her team to score points. If 1A wins the jumble, go to student 2A and give him/her a clue. He/she must give you the correct word which matches that clue. If he/she does, Team A scores a point, and you give student 3A a clue for which you expect

another correct response. Continue giving Team A clues until some team member makes an incorrect response. An incorrect response sends the game back to the jumbled-word face off, this time with students 2A and 2B. Instead of repeating giving clues to the first few students of each team, continue with the student after the one who gave the last incorrect response on the team.

8. Take on the persona of "The Answer Person." Allow students to ask any question about the book. Answer the questions, or tell students where to look in the book to find the answer.

9. Students may enjoy playing charades with events from the story. Select a student to start. Give him/her a card with a scene or event from the story. Allow the players to use their books to find the scene being described. The first person to guess each charade performs the next one.

10. Play a categories-type quiz game. (A master is included in this Unit Plan). Make an overhead transparency of the categories form. Divide the class into teams of three or four players each. Have each team choose a recorder and a banker. choose a team to go first. That team will choose a category and point amount. Ask the question to the entire class.(Use the Study Guide Quiz and Vocabulary questions.) Give the teams one minute to discuss the answer and write it down. Walk around the room and check the answers. Each team that answers correctly receives the points. (Incorrect answers are not penalized; they just don't receive any points). Cross out that square on the playing board. Play continues until all squares have been used. The winning team is the one with the most points. You can assign bonus points to any square or squares you choose.

11. Have students complete the last column (What I Learned) of the KWL sheet you distributed in Lesson One. Discuss their answers with the class.

NOTE: If students do not need the extra review, omit this lesson and go on to the test.

QUIZ GAME
Their Eyes Were Watching God

1-4	5-6	7-11	12-15	16-18	19-20
100	100	100	100	100	100
200	200	200	200	200	200
300	300	300	300	300	300
400	400	400	400	400	400
500	500	500	500	500	500

LESSON NINETEEN

Objective
To test the students' understanding of the main ideas and themes in *Their Eyes Were Watching God*

Activity #1
Distribute the *Their Eyes Were Watching God.* Unit Tests. Go over the instructions in detail and allow the students the entire class period to complete the exam.

Activity #2
Collect all test papers and assigned books prior to the end of the class period.

NOTES ABOUT THE UNIT TESTS IN THIS UNIT:

There are 5 different unit tests which follow.

There are two short answer tests which are based primarily on facts from the novel. The answer key short answer unit test 1 follows the student test. The answer key for short answer test 2 follows the student short answer unit test 2.

There is one advanced short answer unit test. It is based on the extra discussion questions. Use the matching key for short answer unit test 2 to check the matching section of the advanced short answer unit test. There is no key for the short answer questions. The answers will be based on the discussions you have had during class.

There are two multiple choice unit tests. Following the two unit tests, you will find an answer sheet on which students should mark their answers. The same answer sheet should be used for both tests; however, students' answers will be different for each test. Following the students' answer sheet for the multiple choice tests you will find your answer keys.

The short answer tests have a vocabulary section. You should choose 10 of the vocabulary words from this unit, read them orally and have the students write them down. Then, either have students write a definition or use the words in sentences.

UNIT TESTS

SHORT ANSWER UNIT TEST 1 *Their Eyes Were Watching God*

I. Matching/ Identify

1. Eatonville
2. headrags
3. Janie Mae Crawford
4. Joe Starks
5. Logan Killicks
6. de muck
7. Phoeby Watson
8. rabies
9. store
10. Tea Cake

A. central character of story
B. Nanny made Janie marry him for security
C. disease Tea Cake got while fighting a dog
D. heard Janie's story first
E. Son of the Evening Sun, according to Janie
F. Jody made Janie wear them in the store
G. Janie liked its entertainment but not its work
H. town where Jody and Janie settled
I. Janie ran off with him while still married
J. crop land in the Everglades

II. Short Answer

1. What was Janie's idea of love before she was married?

2. What actions did Joe take when he got to Eatonville?

Short Answer Unit Test 1 *Their Eyes Were Watching God*

3. What was the "rock" against which Janie was battered?

4. Discuss the argument between Joe and Janie that started when she incorrectly cut the plug of tobacco. What happened, what did they say to each other, and what was the real reason or the argument?

5. Janie told Phoeby her opinion of remarrying, and of mourning and grief. Discuss what she said about each of them.

6. What was Janie's response when Phoeby talked to her about Tea Cake?

Short Answer Unit Test 1 *Their Eyes Were Watching God*

7. How did Janie feel about her life with Tea Cake?

8. Describe what was happening when the author used the sentence: "They seemed to be staring at the dark, but their eyes were watching God."

9. What happened in the middle of Janie and Tea Cake's fourth week back on the muck after the hurricane? Describe the events in detail.

10. Describe Janie and Tea Cake's last moments together.

Short Answer Unit Test 1 *Their Eyes Were Watching God*

III. Quotations   Identify the speaker and discuss the significance of each of the following quotations.

1. "So when we looked at de picture and everybody got pointed out there wasn't nobody left except a real dark little girl with long hair standing by Eleanore. Dat's where Ah wuz s'posed to be, but Ah couldn't recognize dat dark chile as me. So Ah ast, 'where is me? Ah don't see me.' "

2. "Naw. We been tuhgether round two years. If you kin see de light at daybreak, you don't keer if you die at dusk. It's so many people never see de light at all. Ah wuz fumblin' round and God opened de door."

3. "But nothing can't stop you from wishin'. You can't beat nobody down so low till you can rob 'em of they will.

4. "Somebody got to think for women and chillun and chickens and cows. I god, they sho don't think none theirselves."

5 "Naw, Ah needs two mules dis yeah. Taters is goin' tuh be taters in de fall. Bringin' in big prices. Ah aims tuh run two plows, and dis man Ah'm talkin' 'bout is got uh mule all gentled up so even uh woman kin handle 'im."

Short Answer Unit Test 1 *Their Eyes Were Watching God*

IV. Essay
Compare and contrast Janie's three husbands, and the relationship she had with each of them.

Short Answer Unit Test 1 *Their Eyes Were Watching God*

V. Vocabulary

Write down the vocabulary words your teacher says. Then go back and write down the correct definition for each word.

1. _____

2. _____

3. _____

4. _____

5. _____

6. _____

7. _____

8. _____

9. _____

10. _____

ANSWER KEY SHORT ANSWER UNIT TEST 1 *Their Eyes Were Watching God*

I. Matching/ Identify

H.	1.	Eatonville	A.	central character of story
F.	2.	headrags	B.	Nanny made Janie marry him for security
A.	3.	Janie Mae Crawford	C.	disease Tea Cake got while fighting a dog
I.	4.	Joe Starks	D.	heard Janie's story first
B.	5.	Logan Killicks	E.	Son of the Evening Sun, according to Janie
J.	6.	de muck	F.	Jody made Janie wear them in the store
D.	7.	Phoeby Watson	G.	Janie liked its entertainment but not its work
C.	8	rabies	H.	town where Jody and Janie settled
G.	9.	store	I.	Janie ran off with him while still married
E.	10.	Tea Cake	J.	crop land in the Everglades

II. Short Answer

1. What was Janie's idea of love before she was married?
   She thought she would grow to love her husband, because husbands and wives always loved each other.

2. What actions did Joe take when he got to town?
   He paid cash for 200 acres of land. He opened a store and a post office. He bought the town's first street lamp. He organized the men and built a road. He had a drainage ditch built.

3. What was the "rock" against which Janie was battered?
   She was frustrated in the store when she had to deal with the math involved in the customers' purchases. Joe said she could do it if she wanted to, and he wanted her to use her privileges.

4. Discuss the argument between Joe and Janie that started when she incorrectly cut the plug of tobacco. What happened, what did they say to each other, and what was the real reason for the argument?
   Joe realized he wasn't as young as he used to be. He started picking on Janie because of his fear about his own aging. When she cut the tobacco incorrectly, he used it as another excuse to make fun of her age and her changing physical appearance. This comment, "Don't stand dere rollin' yo' pop eyes at me wid yo' rump hangin' nearly to yo' knees," was meant to amuse the other men and take the focus off of his own fear of aging. Janie retaliated this time: "Yeah, a'hm nearly forty and you's already fifty. How come you can't talk about dat sometimes instead of always pointin' at me?" Joe kept up his insults, and Janie replied: "Taklkin' about me lookin' old! When you pull down yo' britches, you look lak de change uh life." This remark caused Joe great embarrassment. and their relationship took a turn for the worse.

5. Janie told Phoeby her opinion of remarrying, and of mourning and grief. Discuss what she said about each of them.

   Janie didn't want to remarry. She said that Joe had only been dead two months, she had not even given remarriage a thought. A few months later, during another discussion, Janie told Phoeby she liked her new freedom. She also said that mourning should not last longer than grief.

6. What was Janie's response when Phoeby talked to her about Tea Cake?

   She said that she had always wanted to do the things that she was doing with Tea Cake, but Joe would not let her.

7. How did Janie feel about her life with Tea Cake?

   She enjoyed the work and the social life. She liked being able to listen and laugh and talk during the card and dice games.

8. Describe what was happening when the author used the sentence: "They seemed to be staring at the dark, but their eyes were watching God."

   The people who had stayed on the muck were looking out at the hurricane. The wind had just put out the light. They were worried, some wondering if God was going to measure his might against their lack of it.

9. What happened in the middle of Janie and Tea Cake's fourth week back on the muck after the hurricane? Describe the events in detail.

   Tea Cake came home complaining of a headache. He later developed a fever, and his throat closed up so that he could not swallow anything, even water. Janie got the doctor. After examining Tea Cake and listening to them recount the incident with the dog, the doctor told Janie that Tea Cake had rabies. He also said that Tea Cake would have recovered it he had gotten the serum right away, but now it was too late, and he would most likely die.

10. Describe Janie and Tea Cake's last moments together.

    Tea Cake returned from the outhouse with a strange walk, swinging his head from side to side with his jaws clenched. He came into the house and started to fuss at her for not sleeping with him. Janie reminded him that the doctor had told her not to, but Tea Cake would not be appeased. He aimed the pistol at Janie and shot. The first cylinder was empty because Janie had changed it. She loaded her rifle and took aim. They both shot, and Janie killed Tea Cake. She tried to hold him as he fell, and he bit her in the forearm.

Answer Key Short Answer Unit Test 1 *Their Eyes Were Watching God*

III. Quotations

1. "So when we looked at de picture and everybody got pointed out there wasn't nobody left except a real dark little girl with long hair standing by Eleanore. Sat's where Ah wuz s'posed to be, but Ah couldn't recognize dat dark chile as me. So Ah ast, 'where is me? Ah don't see me.' "
    Janie was talking to Phoebe, relating an incident that happened to her as a child. Nanny worked for a white family, and Janie grew up playing with the children in the family. She didn't realize she was black until she saw the picture.

2. "Naw. We been tuhgether round two years. If you kin see de light at daybreak, you don't keer if you die at dusk. It's so many people never see de light at all. Ah wuz fumblin' round and God opened de door."
    Janie was responding to Tea Cake's question . They were in the midst of the hurricane, and he had asked her if she regretted coming to the muck with him.

3. "But nothing can't stop you from wishin'. You can't beat nobody down so low till you can rob 'em of they will."
    Nanny was talking to Janie, explaining her own early life, and her reasons for wanting Janie to marry Logan Killicks.

4. "Somebody got to think for women and chillun and chickens and cows. I god, they sho don't think none theirselves."
    Joe was criticizing Janie in the store. He needed the paperwork for an order, and was blaming Janie because he could not find it.

5 "Naw, Ah needs two mules dis yeah. Taters is goin' tuh be taters in de fall. Bringin' in big prices. Ah aims tuh run two plows, and dis man Ah'm talkin' 'bout is got uh mule all gentled up so even uh woman kin handle 'im."
    Logan Killicks was telling Janie about his plans for the farm, and her role in the plans..

SHORT ANSWER UNIT TEST 2 *Their Eyes Were Watching God*

I. Matching/ Identify

1. Eatonville
2. headrags
3. Janie Mae Crawford
4. Joe Starks
5. Logan Killicks
6. de muck
7. Phoeby Watson
8. rabies
9. store
10. Tea Cake

A. town where Jody and Janie settled
B. Janie liked its entertainment but not its work
C. crop land in the Everglades
D. Son of the Evening Sun, according to Janie
E. Nanny made Janie marry him for security
F. central character of story
G. heard Janie's story first
H. Jody made Janie wear them in the store
I. disease Tea Cake got while fighting a dog
J. Janie ran off with him while still married

II. Short Answer

1. Describe what was happening when the author used the sentence: "They seemed to be staring at the dark, but their eyes were watching God."

2. What happened to Janie and Joe's relationship during the seventh year of their marriage, and why?

Short Answer Unit Test 2 *Their Eyes Were Watching God*

3. What were the main concerns Janie had about getting into a relationship with Tea Cake?

4. Discuss Janie's idea of love before she was married, and how it changed after she had been married for a while.

5. What actions did Joe take when he first arrived in Eatonville? Discuss the results of those actions.

6. Describe Janie's life with Tea Cake.

Short Answer Unit Test 2 *Their Eyes Were Watching God*

7. Describe Janie and Tea Cake's last moments together, starting with Tea Cake pointing the pistol at Janie.

8. What was the real reason behind the argument between Joe and Janie that started when she incorrectly cut the plug of tobacco?

9. What was the "rock" against which Janie was battered?

10. Summarize the events that took place during Janie's trial.

Short Answer Unit Test 2 *Their Eyes Were Watching God*

III. Quotations

Identify the speaker and discuss the significance of each of the following quotations.

1. "But nothing can't stop you from wishin'. You can't beat nobody down so low till you can rob 'em of they will."

2. "Somebody got to think for women and chillun and chickens and cows. I god, they sho don't think none theirselves."

3. "So when we looked at de picture and everybody got pointed out there wasn't nobody left except a real dark little girl with long hair standing by Eleanore. Sat's where Ah wuz s'posed to be, but Ah couldn't recognize dat dark chile as me. So Ah ast, 'where is me? Ah don't see me.' "

4. "Naw, Ah needs two mules dis yeah. Taters is goin' tuh be taters in de fall. Bringin' in big prices. Ah aims tuh run two plows, and dis man Ah'm talkin' 'bout is got uh mule all gentled up so even uh woman kin handle 'im."

5. "Naw. We been tuhgether round two years. If you kin see de light at daybreak, you don't keer if you die at dusk. It's so many people never see de light at all. Ah wuz fumblin' round and God opened de door."

Short Answer Unit Test 2 *Their Eyes Were Watching God*

IV. Essay

Discuss Janie's emergence as a person, and the roles that her three husbands had in her development.

ANSWER KEY SHORT ANSWER UNIT TEST 2 *Their Eyes Were Watching God*
Use this answer key for Short Answer Unit Test 2 and the Advanced Short Answer Unit Test.

I. Matching/Identify

A.	1.	Eatonville	A.	town where Jody and Janie settled
H.	2.	headrags	B.	Janie liked its entertainment but not its work
F.	3.	Janie Mae Crawford	C.	crop land in the Everglades
J.	4.	Joe Starks	D.	Son of the Evening Sun, according to Janie
E.	5.	Logan Killicks	E.	Nanny made Janie marry him for security
C.	6.	de muck	F.	central character of story
G.	7.	Phoeby Watson	G.	heard Janie's story first
I.	8	rabies	H.	Jody made Janie wear them in the store
B.	9.	store	I.	disease Tea Cake got while fighting a dog
D.	10.	Tea Cake	J.	Janie ran off with him while still married

II. Short Answer

1. Describe what was happening when the author used the sentence: "They seemed to be staring at the dark, but their eyes were watching God."

    The people who had stayed on the muck were looking out at the hurricane. The wind had just put out the light. They were worried, some wondering if God was going to measure his might against their lack of it.

2. What happened to Janie and Joe's relationship during the seventh year of their marriage, and why?

    Joe started criticizing Janie. At first she fought back, but she gradually submitted outwardly. She learned to keep her thoughts to herself.

3. What were the main concerns Janie had about getting into a relationship with Tea Cake?

    He was twelve years younger than she was. He didn't look like he had much money. She wasn't sure his intentions were serious.

4. Discuss Janie's idea of love before she was married, and how it changed after she had been married for a while.

    She thought she would grow to love her husband, because husbands and wives always loved each other. After a while with Logan, she discovered that marriage did not make love.

Answer Key Short Answer Unit Test 2 *Their Eyes Were Watching God*

5. What actions did Joe take when he first arrived in Eatonville? Discuss the results of those actions.

   He paid cash for 200 acres of land. He opened a store and a post office. He bought the town's first street lamp. He organized the men and built a road. He had a drainage ditch built. When he suggest that the town incorporate and elect a mayor, he was elected.

6. Describe Janie's life with Tea Cake.

   She enjoyed the work and the social life. She liked being able to listen and laugh and talk during the card and dice games. She went with him each day to pick beans, and they made supper together. They played and generally lifted the spirits of those around them. Tea Cake taught her to shoot, and they went hunting together. At night, their house was the center of the social life.

7. Describe Janie and Tea Cake's last moments together, starting with Tea Cake pointing the pistol at Janie.

   Tea Cake returned from the outhouse with a strange walk, swinging his head from side to side with his jaws clenched. He came into the house and started to fuss at her for not sleeping with him. Janie reminded him that the doctor had told her not to, but Tea Cake would not be appeased. He aimed the pistol at Janie and shot. The first cylinder was empty because Janie had changed it. She loaded her rifle and took aim. They both shot, and Janie killed Tea Cake. She tried to hold him as he fell, and he bit her in the forearm.

8. What was the real reason behind the argument between Joe and Janie that started when she incorrectly cut the plug of tobacco?

   Joe realized he wasn't as young as he used to be. He started picking on Janie because of his fear about his own aging. When she cut the tobacco incorrectly, he used it as another excuse to make fun of her age and her changing physical appearance. This comment, "Don't stand dere rollin' yo' pop eyes at me wid yo' rump hangin' nearly to yo' knees," was meant to amuse the other men and take the focus off of his own fear of aging. Janie retaliated this time: "Yeah, a'hm nearly forty and you's already fifty. How come you can't talk about dat sometimes instead of always pointin' at me?" Joe kept up his insults, and Janie replied: "Talkin' about me lookin' old! When you pull down yo' britches, you look lak de change uh life. "This remark caused Joe great embarrassment. and their relationship took a turn for the worse.

9. What was the "rock" against which Janie was battered?

   She was frustrated in the store when she had to deal with the math involved in the customers' purchases. Joe said she could do it id she wanted to, and he wanted her to use her privileges.

10. Summarize the events that took place during Janie's trial.

   Janie was tried the same day she shot Tea Cake. The jury was composed of twelve white men. The colored people were lining the walls in the back of the courtroom. She felt that they were all against her. Some of them sent word to the prosecutor that they wanted to testify, but their request was not granted. The sheriff and the doctor testified about what Janie did immediately after the shooting. The doctor also told the court about the rabies, and how he found Janie with Tea Cake in her arms. Then Janie took the stand and told what had happened. The jury found her innocent.

III. Quotations

1. "But nothing can't stop you from wishin'. You can't beat nobody down so low till you can rob 'em of they will.

   Nanny was talking to Janie, explaining her own early life, and her reasons for wanting Janie to marry Logan Killicks.

2. "Somebody got to think for women and chillun and chickens and cows. I god, they sho don't think none theirselves."

   Joe was criticizing Janie in the store. He needed the paperwork for an order, and was blaming Janie because he could not find it.

3. "So when we looked at de picture and everybody got pointed out there wasn't nobody left except a real dark little girl with long hair standing by Eleanore. Dat's where Ah wuz s'posed to be, but Ah couldn't recognize dat dark chile as me. So Ah ast, 'where is me? Ah don't see me.' "

   Janie was talking to Phoebe, relating an incident that happened to her as a child. Nanny worked for a white family, and Janie grew up playing with the children in the family. She didn't realize she was black until she saw the picture.

4. "Naw, Ah needs two mules dis yeah. Taters is goin' tuh be taters in de fall. Bringin' in big prices. Ah aims tuh run two plows, and dis man Ah'm talkin' 'bout is got uh mule all gentled up so even uh woman kin handle 'im."

   Logan Killicks was telling Janie about his plans for the farm, and her role in the plans..

5 "Naw. We been tuhgether round two years. If you kin see de light at daybreak, you don't keer if you die at dusk. It's so many people never see de light at all. Ah wuz fumblin' round and God opened de door."

   Janie was responding to Tea Cake's question. They were in the midst of the hurricane, and he had asked her if she regretted coming to the muck with him.

ADVANCED SHORT ANSWER UNIT TEST *Their Eyes Were Watching God*

I. Matching/ Identify

1. Eatonville
2. headrags
3. Janie Mae Crawford
4. Joe Starks
5. Logan Killicks
6. de muck
7. Phoeby Watson
8. rabies
9. store
10. Tea Cake

A. town where Jody and Janie settled
B. Janie liked its entertainment but not its work
C. crop land in the Everglades
D. Son of the Evening Sun, according to Janie
E. Nanny made Janie marry him for security
F. central character of story
G. heard Janie's story first
H. Jody made Janie wear them in the store
I. disease Tea Cake got while fighting a dog
J. Janie ran off with him while still married

II. Short Answer

1. Discuss Janie's emergence as a person, and the roles that her three husbands had in her development.

Advanced Short Answer Unit Test *Their Eyes Were Watching God*

2. Discuss the symbolism in the use of the horizon in the novel.

3. Discuss the symbolic importance of the mule and "mule talk" in the novel.

Advanced Short Answer Unit Test *Their Eyes Were Watching God*

4. Discuss the significance of the muck dwellers' reaction to the oncoming hurricane, and Hurston's statement: "They seemed to be staring at the dark, but their eyes were watching God."

5. Which of the following placed the most limits on Janie-race, sex, class, or the attitudes of others? Support your answer with examples from the novel.

Advanced Short Answer Unit Test *Their Eyes Were Watching God*

III. Quotations
    Identify the speaker and discuss the significance of each quotation.

1. "So when we looked at de picture and everybody got pointed out there wasn't nobody left except a real dark little girl with long hair standing by Eleanort. Sat's where Ah wuz s'posed to be, but Ah couldn't recognize dat dark chile as me. So Ah ast, 'where is me? Ah don't see me.' "

2. "Naw. We been tuhgether round two years. If you kin see de light at daybreak, you don't keer if you die at dusk. It's so many people never see de light at all. Ah wuz fumblin' round and God opened de door."

3. "But nothing can't stop you from wishin'. You can't beat nobody down so low till you can rob 'em of they will."

4. "Somebody got to think for women and chillun and chickens and cows. I god, they sho don't think none theirselves."

5 "Naw, Ah needs two mules dis yeah. Taters is goin' tuh be taters in de fall. Bringin' in big prices. Ah aims tuh run two plows, and dis man Ah'm talkin' 'bout is got uh mule all gentled up so even uh woman kin handle 'im."

Advanced Short Answer Unit Test *Their Eyes Were Watching God*

III. Quotations
  Identify the speaker and discuss the significance of each quotation.

6. "Ah knowed you wasn't going tuh lissen tuh me. You changes everything but nothin' don't change you-not even death."

7. "Janie, Ah hope god may kill me, if Ah'm lyin'. Nobody else on earth kin hold uh candle tuh you, baby. You got de keys to de kingdom."

8. "Ah don't want yo' feathers always crumpled by folks throwin' up things in yo' face. And Ah can't die easy thinkin' maybe de menfolks white or black is makin' a spittin' cup outa you. Have some sympathy fuh me. Put me down easy, Janie, Ah'm a cracked plate."

9. "Thanky, Ma'am. But 'sposing you wuz tuh die, now. You wouldn't git mad at me for draggin' yuh heah?"

10. "Lawd! Ah done growed ten feet higher from jus' listenin' tuh you, Janie. Ah ain't satisfied wid mahself no mo'. "

Advanced Short Answer Unit Test *Their Eyes Were Watching God*

IV. Vocabulary

Listen to the words and write them down. After you have written down all of the words, write a paragraph in which you use all the words. The paragraph must in some way relate to *Their Eyes Were Watching God*.

Answer Key Advanced Short Answer Unit Test *Their Eyes Were Watching God*

III. Quotations

1. "So when we looked at de picture and everybody got pointed out there wasn't nobody left except a real dark little girl with long hair standing by Eleanort. Dat's where Ah wuz s'posed to be, but Ah couldn't recognize dat dark chile as me. So Ah ast, 'where is me? Ah don't see me.' "

    Janie was talking to Phoebe, relating an incident that happened to her as a child. Nanny worked for a white family, and Janie grew up playing with the children in the family. She didn't realize she was black until she saw the picture.

2. "Naw. We been tuhgether round two years. If you kin see de light at daybreak, you don't keer if you die at dusk. It's so many people never see de light at all. Ah wuz fumblin' round and God opened de door."

    Janie was responding to Tea Cake's question . They were in the midst of the hurricane, and he had asked her if she regretted coming to the muck with him.

3. "But nothing can't stop you from wishin'. You can't beat nobody down so low till you can rob 'em of they will."

    Nanny was talking to Janie, explaining her own early life, and her reasons for wanting Janie to marry Logan Killicks.

4. "Somebody got to think for women and chillun and chickens and cows. I god, they sho don't think none theirselves."

    Joe was criticizing Janie in the store. He needed the paperwork for an order, and was blaming Janie because he could not find it.

5. "Naw, Ah needs two mules dis yeah. Taters is goin' tuh be taters in de fall. Bringin' in big prices. Ah aims tuh run two plows, and dis man Ah'm talkin' 'bout is got uh mule all gentled up so even uh woman kin handle 'im."

    Logan Killicks was telling Janie about his plans for the farm ,and her role in the plans.

6. "Ah knowed you wasn't going tuh lissen tuh me. You changes everything but nothin' don't change you-not even death."

    Janie was talking to Joe as he lay dying. He didn't want to listen to her, and had just told her to leave the room.

7. "Janie, Ah hope God may kill me, if Ah'm lyin'. Nobody else on earth kin hold uh candle tuh you, baby. You got de keys to de kingdom."

    Janie was questioning Tea Cake's intentions toward her after he invited her to attend the Sunday School picnic with him.

8. "Ah don't want yo' feathers always crumpled by folks throwin' up things in yo' face. And Ah can't die easy thinkin' maybe de menfolks white or black is makin' a spittin' cup outa you. Have some sympathy fuh me. Put me down easy, Janie, Ah'm a cracked plate."

    Nanny was explaining her reasons for wanting Janie to get married.

9. "Thanky, Ma'am. But 'sposing you wuz tuh die, now. You wouldn't git mad at me for draggin' yuh heah?"

    Tea Cake and Janie were in the midst of the hurricane. Tea Cake was unsure whether or not Janie still wanted to be with him.

10. "Lawd! Ah done growed ten feet higher from jus' listenin' tuh you, Janie. Ah ain't satisfied wid mahself no mo'. "

    This was Phoeby's comment as Janie finished telling her the story.

MULTIPLE CHOICE UNIT TEST 1 *Their Eyes Were Watching God*

I. Matching/Identification
1. Eatonville
2. headrags
3. Janie Mae Crawford
4. Joe Starks
5. Logan Killicks
6. de muck
7. Phoeby Watson
8. rabies
9. store
10. Tea Cake

A. central character of story
B. Nanny made Janie marry him for security
C. disease Tea Cake got while fighting a dog
D. heard Janies's story first
E. Son of the Evening Sun, according to Janie
F. Jody made Janie wear them in the store
G. Janie liked its entertainment but not its work
H. town where Jody and Janie settled
I. Janie ran off with him while still married
J. crop land in the Everglades

II. Multiple Choice

1. True or False: Janie thought she would grow to love her husband, because husbands and wives always loved each other.
    A. True
    B. False

2. Which of the following is **not** something Joe did when he got to town?
    A. He bought the town's first automobile.
    B. He paid cash for 200 acres of land.
    C. He opened a store and a post office. He bought the town's first street lamp.
    D. He organized the men to build a road and a drainage ditch.

3. True or False: Janie was frustrated with trying to do the math required of her in the store.
    A. True
    B. False

4. True or False: Janie loved her new freedom.
    A. True
    B. False

5. What did Janie say about mourning and grief?
    A. She said they should both last for the same amount of time as one had known the person.
    B. She said they should not be expressed publicly.
    C. She said she mourned for Joe but grieved for herself.
    D. She said mourning shouldn't last any longer than grief.

Multiple Choice Unit Test 1 *Their Eyes Were Watching God*

6. What was Janie's response when Phoeby talked to her about Tea Cake?
    A. She said she was just having a fling for fun, but she was not serious about him.
    B. She got angry and told Phoeby to mind her own business.
    C. She said she had always wanted to go and do the things that she was doing with Tea Cake, but that Joe wouldn't let her.
    D. She said she thought a little bit of attention was good for business in the store.

7. Why did Janie start to go out and pick beans?
    A. They needed the money.
    B. She didn't trust Tea Cake among all of the other women.
    C. Tea Cake asked her to because he was lonely without her.
    D. The foreman said she had to or she couldn't live in the company house anymore.

8. True or False: When the author used the sentence "They seemed to be staring at the dark, but their eyes were watching God," the people were in church during a candle-light service.
    A. True
    B. False

9. What did Janie do after the doctor left?
    A. She went outside and looked up at the sky. She wondered if God was noticing what was going on, and if he had intentionally caused this problem for her and Tea Cake.
    B. She asked the doctor find a good hospital for Tea Cake. She said she had plenty of money to pay for the best care possible.
    C. She wrote a letter to Phoeby and asked her to come and help her take Tea Cake home.
    D. She went to see the minister and asked him why bad things had to happen to good people.

10. What happened just before Tea Cake died?
    A. Tea Cake bit Janie on the arm.
    B. Tea Cake regained his senses and told her he loved her.
    C. He tried to strangle Janie.
    D. Janie tried to shoot herself, but the pistol was empty.

Multiple Choice Unit Test 1 *Their Eyes Were Watching God*

III. Quotations   Identify the speaker:

    A. Janie   C. Logan Killicks   E. Nanny
    B. Joe Starks   D. Tea Cake   F. Phoeby

1. "So when we looked at de picture and everybody got pointed out there wasn't nobody left except a real dark little girl with long hair standing by Eleanort. Sat's where Ah wuz s'posed to be, but Ah couldn't recognize dat dark chile as me. So Ah ast, 'where is me? Ah don't see me.' "

2. "Naw. We been tuhgether round two years. If you kin see de light at daybreak, you don't keer if you die at dusk. It's so many people never see de light at all. Ah wuz fumblin' round and God opened de door."

3. "But nothing can't stop you from wishin'. You can't beat nobody down so low till you can rob 'em of they will."

4. "Somebody got to think for women and chillun and chickens and cows. I god, they sho don't think none theirselves."

5. "Naw, Ah needs two mules dis yeah. Taters is goin' tuh be taters in de fall. Bringin' in big prices. Ah aims tuh run two plows, and dis man Ah'm talkin' 'bout is got uh mule all gentled up so even uh woman kin handle 'im."

6. "Ah knowed you wasn't going tuh lissen tuh me. You changes everything but nothin' don't change you—not even death."

7. "Janie, Ah hope god may kill me, if Ah'm lyin'. Nobody else on earth kin hold uh candle tuh you, baby. You got de keys to de kingdom."

8. "Ah don't want yo' feathers always crumpled by folks throwin' up things in yo' face. And Ah can't die easy thinkin' maybe de menfolks white or black is makin' a spittin' cup outa you. Have some sympathy fuh me. Put me down easy, Janie, Ah'm a cracked plate."

9. "Thanky, Ma'am. But 'sposing you wuz tuh die, now. You wouldn't git mad at me for draggin' yuh heah?"

10. "Lawd! Ah done growed ten feet higher from jus' listenin' tuh you, Janie. Ah ain't satisfied wid mahself no mo'. "

Multiple Choice Unit Test 1 *Their Eyes Were Watching God*

IV. Vocabulary Matching

1. resignation
2. languid
3. expound
4. mien
5. sauntered
6. cowed
7. sullen
8. prostrating
9. futile
10. refracted
11. excruciating
12. languished
13. hypocrites
14. predecessor
15. sacrilege
16. stolid
17. cosmic
18. compellment
19. lustily
20. delirium

A. strong forces
B. against something sacred
C. wasted away; weakened
D. having no useful result
E. bullied
F. explain; give a detailed account
G. mental confusion caused by illness
H. ancestor; forebearer
I. light deflected from a straight path
J. manner or appearance
K. unresisting acceptance
L. universal; vast
M. intensely painful; agonizing
N. bowing in adoration or submission
O. robustly; strongly
P. morose or sulky
Q. people who say one thing but do another
R. having or showing little or no emotion
S. strolled
T. lacking energy or vitality; weak

MULTIPLE CHOICE UNIT TEST 2 *Their Eyes Were Watching God*

I. Matching/ Identify

1. Eatonville
2. headrags
3. Janie Mae Crawford
4. Joe Starks
5. Logan Killicks
6. de muck
7. Phoeby Watson
8. rabies
9. store
10. Tea Cake

A. town where Jody and Janie settled
B. Janie liked its entertainment but not its work
C. crop land in the Everglades
D. Son of the Evening Sun, according to Janie
E. Nanny made Janie marry him for security
F. central character of story
G. heard Janie's story first
H. Jody made Janie wear them in the store
I. disease Tea Cake got while fighting a dog
J. Janie ran off with him while still married

Multiple Choice Unit Test 2 *Their Eyes Were Watching God*

II. Multiple Choice

1. True or False: When the author used the sentence "They seemed to be staring at the dark, but their eyes were watching God," the people were in church during a candle-light service.
    A. True
    B. False

2. What happened to Joe and Janie's relationship during the seventh year of their marriage?
    A. It got better than it ever had been. Joe started complimenting her and buying her gifts.
    B. Janie began making fun of Joe for things he did.
    C. Janie learned to keep her thoughts to herself instead of fighting Joe's criticism.
    D. Janie wanted a divorce but Joe wouldn't let her get one.

3. Which of the following is **not** one of the main concerns that Janie had about getting into a relationship with Tea Cake?
    A. He was about twelve years younger than she was.
    B. He didn't look like he had much money.
    C. She wasn't sure his intentions were serious or honorable.
    D. She had not been a widow long enough to start another relationship.

4. What did Janie discover about love?
    A. She discovered she was not capable of love.
    B. She discovered she did not like being in love.
    C. She discovered that her initial thoughts about love were correct.
    D. She discovered that marriage did not make love.

5. Which of the following is **not** something Joe did when he got to town?
    A. He bought the town's first automobile.
    B. He paid cash for 200 acres of land.
    C. He opened a store and a post office. He bought the town's first street lamp.
    D. He organized the men to build a road and a drainage ditch.

6. What was Janie's response when Tea Cake asked Janie if she wished she had stayed in her big house, away from dangers such as the hurricane?
    A. She said it was too late to think about those things.
    B. She said she didn't think she would die until her time came, and that she was happy being with Tea Cake.
    C. She said she was looking forward to the adventure.
    D. She said yes, she wished she had, and that she would go back home after the hurricane.

Multiple Choice Unit Test 2 *Their Eyes Were Watching God*

7. What happened just before Tea Cake died?
    A. Tea Cake bit Janie on the arm.
    B. Tea Cake regained his senses and told her he loved her.
    C. He tried to strangle Janie.
    D. Janie tried to shoot herself, but the pistol was empty.

8. What was the real reason behind the argument between Joe and Janie that started with her incorrectly cutting the plug of tobacco?
    A. Joe realized he wasn't as young as he used to be. He started picking on Janie because of his fear about his own aging.
    B. Joe was jealous. He thought she was giving Steve Mixon extra tobacco because she was secretly in love with him.
    C. He was furious because she was losing money for the store.
    D. He liked it that she was helpless and ineffective, because it made him look competent and generous to the customers.

9. True or False: Janie was frustrated with trying to do the math required of her in the store.
    A. True
    B. False

10. What was Janie's reaction when Joe said she couldn't make a speech?
    A. She felt cold; his remarks took the bloom off things.
    B. She was glad, because she didn't want to make a speech.
    (Two choices only)

Multiple Choice Unit Test 2 *Their Eyes Were Watching God*

III. Quotations   Identify the speaker:

    A. Janie   C. Logan Killicks   E. Nanny
    B. Joe Starks   D. Tea Cake   F. Phoeby

1. " 'Cause you told me Ah mus gointer love him, and, Ah don't. Maybe if somebody was to tell me how, Ah could do it."

2. "Naw. We been tuhgether round two years. If you kin see de light at daybreak, you don't keer if you die at dusk. It's so many people never see de light at all. Ah wuz fumblin' round and God opened de door."

3. "Lawd! Ah done growed ten feet higher from jus' listenin' tuh you, Janie. Ah ain't satisfied wid mahself no mo'. "

4. "Somebody got to think for women and chillun and chickens and cows. I god, they sho don't think none theirselves."

5. "If people thinks de same they can make it all right. So in the beginnin' new thoughts had tuh be thought and new words said. After Ah got used tuh dat, we gits 'long jus' fine. He done taught me de maiden language all over.'

6. "Naw, Jody, it wasn't because Ah didn't have no sympathy. Ah had uh lavish uh dat. Ah just didn't never git no chance tuh use none of it. You wouldn't let me."

7. "Janie, Ah hope god may kill me, if Ah'm lyin'. Nobody else on earth kin hold uh candle tuh you, baby. You got de keys to de kingdom."

8. "But nothing can't stop you from wishin'. You can't beat nobody down so low till you can rob 'em of they will."

9. "Thanky, Ma'am. But 'sposing you wuz tuh die, now. You wouldn't git mad at me for draggin' yuh heah?"

10. "Naw, Ah needs two mules dis yeah. Taters is goin' tuh be taters in de fall. Bringin' in big prices. Ah aims tuh run two plows, and dis man Ah'm talkin' 'bout is got uh mule all gentled up so even uh woman kin handle 'im."

Multiple Choice Unit Test 2 *Their Eyes Were Watching God*

IV. Vocabulary

1.	wanton	A.	cruel, merciless
2.	treacherous	B.	area of control
3.	desecrating	C.	subtly made suggestions
4.	broached	D.	a fight; a brawl
5.	jurisdiction	E.	a bad or evil person
6.	eulogy	F.	speech or praise about a dead person
7.	ostentatiously	G.	savageness; fierceness
8.	usurper	H.	not trustworthy; dangerous
9.	temporized	I.	speed
10.	insinuations	J.	one who grabs money or property
11.	endurable	K.	vomited; threw up
12.	dwindled	L.	brought up for discussion
13.	fend	M.	quiet; difficult to detect
14.	subtle	N.	negotiated to gain time
15.	fracas	O.	became gradually smaller
16.	velocity	P.	persistence; dogged trying
17.	perseverance	Q.	in a pompous manner; showing off
18.	disgorged	R.	resist; push away; shield
19.	ferocity	S.	violating the sacredness of
20.	fiend	T.	long lasting; able to be tolerated for a long time

ANSWER SHEET   Multiple Choice Unit Tests   *Their Eyes Were Watching God*

I. Matching	III. Quotations	IV. Vocabulary
1.	1.	1.
2.	2.	2.
3.	3.	3.
4.	4.	4.
5.	5.	5.
6.	6.	6.
7.	7.	7.
8.	8.	8.
9.	9.	9.
10.	10.	10.
		11.
		12.

II. Multiple Choice

1. (A) (B) (C) (D)
2. (A) (B) (C) (D)
3. (A) (B) (C) (D)
4. (A) (B) (C) (D)
5. (A) (B) (C) (D)
6. (A) (B) (C) (D)
7. (A) (B) (C) (D)
8. (A) (B) (C) (D)
9. (A) (B) (C) (D)
10. (A) (B) (C) (D)

13.
14.
15.
16.
17.
18.
19.
20.

ANSWER SHEET KEY   Multiple Choice Unit Test 1   *Their Eyes Were Watching God*

I. Matching		III. Quotations		IV. Vocabulary	
1.	H	1.	A	1.	K
2.	F	2.	A	2.	T
3.	A	3.	E	3.	F
4.	I	4.	B	4.	J
5.	B	5.	C	5.	S
6.	J	6.	A	6.	E
7.	D	7.	D	7.	P
8.	C	8.	E	8.	N
9.	G	9.	D	9.	D
10.	E	10.	F	10.	I
				11.	M
				12.	C
				13.	Q
				14.	H
				15.	B
				16.	R
				17.	L
				18.	A
				19.	O
				20.	G

II. Multiple Choice
1. ( ) (B) (C) (D)
2. ( ) (B) (C) (D)
3. ( ) (B) (C) (D)
4. ( ) (B) (C) (D)
5. (A) (B) (C) ( )
6. (A) (B) ( ) (D)
7. (A) (B) ( ) (D)
8. (A) ( ) (C) (D)
9. ( ) (B) (C) (D)
10. ( ) (B) (C) (D)

ANSWER SHEET KEY   Multiple Choice Unit Test 2 *Their Eyes Were Watching God*

I. Matching
1. A
2. H
3. F
4. J
5. E
6. C
7. G
8. I
9. B
10. D

II. Multiple Choice
1. (A) ( ) (C) (D)
2. (A) (B) ( ) (D)
3. (A) (B) ( ) (D)
4. (A) (B) (C) ( )
5. ( ) (B) (C) (D)
6. (A) ( ) (C) (D)
7. ( ) (B) (C) (D)
8. ( ) (B) (C) (D)
9. ( ) (B) (C) (D)
10. ( ) (B) (C) (D)

III. Quotations
1. A
2. A
3. F
4. B
5. A
6. A
7. D
8. E
9. D
10. C

IV. Vocabulary
1. A
2. H
3. S
4. L
5. B
6. F
7. Q
8. J
9. N
10. C
11. T
12. O
13. R
14. M
15. D
16. I
17. P
18. K
19. G
20. E

UNIT RESOURCE MATERIALS

BULLETIN BOARD IDEAS - *Their Eyes Were Watching God*

1. Save one corner of the board for the best of students' writing assignments. You may want to use background maps of Florida to represent the setting of the novel.

2. Take one of the word search puzzles from the unit resource section and copy it over in a large size on the bulletin board. Write the clue words to find to one side. Invite students prior to and after class to find the words and circle them on the bulletin board.

3. Have students find or draw pictures they think represent people or scenes from the book.

4. Invite students to help make an interactive bulletin board quiz. Give each student a half sheet of paper folded in half so that it can open. On the outside flap, have each student write a description of one of the characters in the text. On the inside, they will write the name of the character. You can staple or tack these papers to the bulletin board so that the students can read the descriptions and lift the flaps to find the answers.

5. Collect pictures or travel information about the cities mentioned in the book.

6. Make book jackets and display them on the bulletin board.

7. Make a display of pictures and articles about hurricanes.

8. Display articles about Zora Neale Hurston and critiques of her work.

9. Have students design postcards depicting the settings of the book.

EXTRA ACTIVITIES - *Their Eyes Were Watching God*

One of the difficulties in teaching a novel is that all students don't read at the same speed. One student who likes to read may take the book home and finish it in a day or two. Sometimes a few students finish the in class assignments early. The problem, then, is finding suitable extra activities for students.

One thing you can do is to keep a little library of related books and magazines in your classroom. For this unit on *Their Eyes Were Watching God*, you might make available other books by Zora Neale Hurston. There are also many other novels by members of the Harlem Renaissance group of writers that students would enjoy reading. The reference department of most libraries has bibliographies of the works of African-American, female writers.

Several African-American writers, including Alice Walker, Toni Morrison, and Ralph Ellison studied the works of Zora Neale Hurston. Students could read works by one or more of these authors and compare them.

Students who enjoyed this novel may be interested in reading Hurston's autobiography.

Consult a doctor or do research on rabies and report to the class.

The novel is available on audio tape. Your students who have reading difficulties or speak English as a second language may benefit from listening to all or part of the book on tape.

A movie version of the novel is available in some commercial video rental stores. Students could watch the movie after reading the novel and compare and contrast them.

Some students may like to draw. You might devise a contest or allow some extra credit grade for students who draw characters or scenes from the novel. Note, too, that if the students do not want to keep their drawings, you may pick up some extra bulletin board materials this way.

Have maps and travel brochures on hand for easy reference. Travel agencies and automobile clubs are good sources of these materials.

Other things you may keep on hand are puzzles. Several puzzles relating directly to this novel are included in this unit. Feel free to duplicate them for your class.

The pages which follow contain games, puzzles, and worksheets. The keys, when appropriate, immediately follow the puzzle or worksheet. There are two main groups of activities: one group for the unit; that is, generally relating to the characters and places and symbols in the text, and another group of activities related primarily to the vocabulary words from the story.

MORE ACTIVITIES - *Their Eyes Were Watching God*

1. Pick one of the incidents for students to dramatize. Encourage students to write dialog for the characters. (Perhaps you could assign various stories to different groups of students so more than one story could be acted and more students could participate.)

2. Have students design a book cover (front and back and inside flaps) for this novel.

3. Have students design a bulletin board (ready to put up; not just sketched) for this novel.

4. Invite a story teller to tell one or more stories related to *Their Eyes Were Watching God.*

5. help students design and produce a talk show. Choose one of the story incidents as the topic. The host will interview the various characters. (Students should make up the questions they want the host to ask the characters.)

6. Have students work in pairs to create an interview with one of the characters. One student should be the interviewer and the other should be the interviewee. Students can work together to compose questions for the interviewer to ask. Each pair of students could present their interview to the class.

7. Invite students who have read other books by Zora Neale Hurston or her autobiography to share what they read the class.

8. Have students hold small group discussions related to topics in the book. Assign a recorder and a speaker for each group. have the speaker from each group make a report to the class.

9. Write another chapter detailing what Janie did next in her life.

10. Contact a local university and find a student or professor who specializes in Black American Literature. Invite the person to speak to the class.

11. Compare and contrast the novel with others that have African-American central characters.

12. Research the life style of migrant farm workers in Florida in the early 1900s.

WORD SEARCH *Their Eyes Were Watching God*

All the words in this list are associated with *Their Eyes Were Watching God* with emphasis on the characters and events being studied in this unit. The words are placed backwards, forward, diagonally, up and down. The words used in the puzzle are listed below.

```
H E Z E K I A H U R R I C A N E Q W E M
A S E L O N I M E S O P H T H L S O A F
I S Z A H D X S G N Y E H C W F J L T S
R Y P I S T O L A A A F A J O I F L O S
M O U R N I N G O D M D S T O R E A N K
P J L T W H O L R Q A B B K D D Y W V N
H N Z T Y L V A X E S N L O S X Y S I O
O W Y S Z N G P H J E U T I O P J X L K
E C A K E S N A E B R N U S N T M U L E
B N C C E N A F C H R K R I B G Y A E C
Y U K I G Y N S V E E I N M H Z M N S H
M T B L D F N C I Z N E E M N P P D Y O
M A G L X Y Y N V L T N R O Q V E G Z B
R N H I D Y A M E D O O C N Y E B Z S E
L S Z K G J Y H Q N R Q C S S Y Q Z M E
```

BEANS	HEZEKIAH	MUCK	SEMINOLES
BOOTYNY	HURRICANE	MULE	SERRENT
CAKE	JANIE	NANNY	SIMMONS
COODEMAY	JODY	NUNKIE	STORE
DOG	JOE	OKECHOBEE	SWALLOW
EATONVILLE	KILLICKS	PHOEBY	TRIAL
GAMBLING	LAMP	PISTOL	TURNER
HAIR	LOGAN	RABIES	WOODS
HEADACHE	MAYOR	RIFLE	
HEADRAGS	MOURNING	SEEDS	

WORD SEARCH ANSWER KEY
Their Eyes Were Watching God

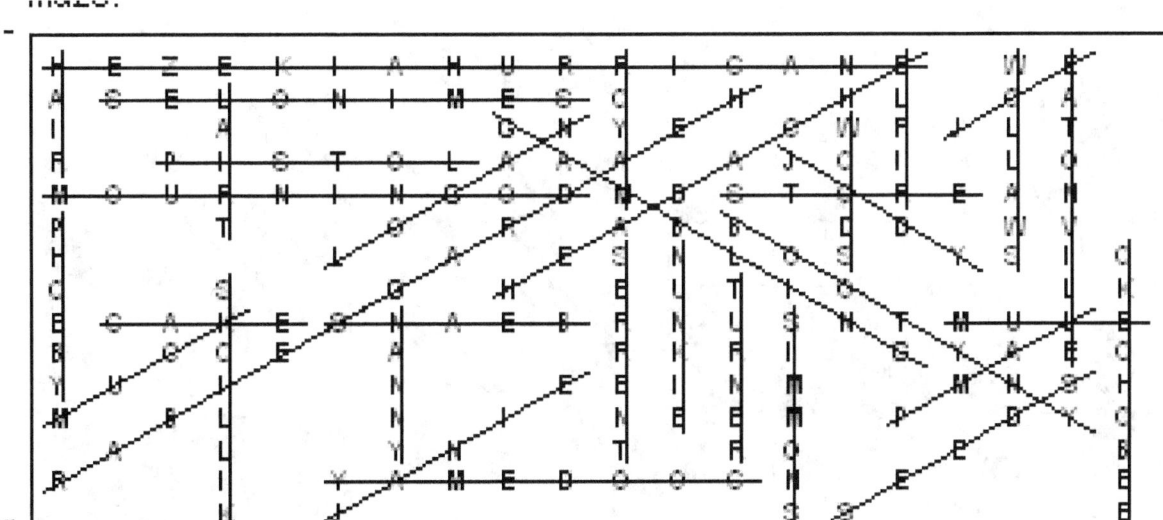

CROSSWORD *Their Eyes Were Watching God*

128

CROSSWORD CLUES *Their Eyes Were Watching God*

ACROSS
1 Tea Cake's weapon
5 Doctor who testified on Janie's behalf
7 Acted like Joe in the store
9 Tea Cake's first symptom
12 Site of Tea Cake and Janie's wedding
16 Narrator of the story
19 Location of the muck
21 Vergible ___; Tea Cake
23 Nanny compared the black woman to one
26 Joe's nickname
27 Raised Janie
28 Held the same day as Tea Cake's death
30 Mrs. ___ didn't like dark-skinned Blacks
31 Crop they picked on the muck
32 Joe started one in Eatonville

DOWN
2 What Tea Cake couldn't do when he was sick
3 Janie brought these back from the muck
4 Last name of Janie's farmer husband
6 What Tea Cake called the Everglade crop land
7 Joe made Janie wear them in the store
8 Caused the evacuation of the muck
9 Janie's most noticeable physical characteristic
10 Tea ___
11 Tea Cake killed it to save Janie
12 Janie's businessman-mayor husband
13 Tea Cake tried to put him out of the restaurant
14 Janie's weapon
15 Threw his coffee cup at Coodemay
17 Joe was the first one in Eatonville
18 Janie watched a band of them leave the muck
19 Town where Joe and Janie settled
20 How Tea Cake got Janie's money back
22 Made a play for Tea Cake
23 Slept through the hurricane
24 Mr. Killicks' first name
25 Drunken instigator of the fight at the restaurant
29 Town celebrated its installation; street ___

CROSSWORD ANSWER KEY
Their Eyes Were Watching God

MATCHING QUIZ/WORKSHEET 1 - Their Eyes Were Watching God

___ 1. NANNY   A. What Tea Cake called the Everglade crop land

___ 2. JOE   B. First to hear Janie's story

___ 3. PHOEBY   C. Town celebrated its installation; street ___

___ 4. STORE   D. Town where Joe and Janie settled

___ 5. JODY   E. Tea Cake killed it to save Janie

___ 6. MAYOR   F. Janie's businessman-mayor husband

___ 7. GAMBLING   G. Narrator of the story

___ 8. RIFLE   H. Janie watched a band of them leave the muck

___ 9. SOP   I. Drunken instigator of fight at the restaurant

___ 10. BEANS   J. Nanny compared the black woman to one

___ 11. HEZEKIAH   K. Joe's nickname

___ 12. TRIAL   L. Slept through the hurricane

___ 13. MUCK   M. Tea Cake's weapon

___ 14. PISTOL   N. Tea Cake tried to put him out of the restaurant

___ 15. SERRENT   O. Joe started one in Eatonville

___ 16. EATONVILLE   P. Mr. Killicks' first name

___ 17. MOTORBOAT   Q. Threw his coffee cup at Coodemay

___ 18. COODEMAY   R. How Tea Cake got Janie's money back

___ 19. LOGAN   S. Raised Janie

___ 20. SEMINOLES   T. Acted like Joe in the store

___ 21. BOOTYNY   U. Janie's weapon

___ 22. MULE   V. Held the same day as Tea Cake's death

___ 23. LAMP   W. Joe was the first one in Eatonville

___ 24. JANIE   X. Wanted to testify at Janie's trial: ___-de-Bottom

___ 25. DOG   Y. Crop they picked on the muck

KEY: MATCHING QUIZ/WORKSHEET 1 - Their Eyes Were Watching God

S - 1. NANNY	A. What Tea Cake called the Everglade crop land
F - 2. JOE	B. First to hear Janie's story
B - 3. PHOEBY	C. Town celebrated its installation; street ___
O - 4. STORE	D. Town where Joe and Janie settled
K - 5. JODY	E. Tea Cake killed it to save Janie
W - 6. MAYOR	F. Janie's businessman-mayor husband
R - 7. GAMBLING	G. Narrator of the story
U - 8. RIFLE	H. Janie watched a band of them leave the muck
X - 9. SOP	I. Drunken instigator of fight at the restaurant
Y -10. BEANS	J. Nanny compared the black woman to one
T -11. HEZEKIAH	K. Joe's nickname
V -12. TRIAL	L. Slept through the hurricane
A -13. MUCK	M. Tea Cake's weapon
M -14. PISTOL	N. Tea Cake tried to put him out of the restaurant
I -15. SERRENT	O. Joe started one in Eatonville
D -16. EATONVILLE	P. Mr. Killicks' first name
L -17. MOTORBOAT	Q. Threw his coffee cup at Coodemay
N -18. COODEMAY	R. How Tea Cake got Janie's money back
P -19. LOGAN	S. Raised Janie
H -20. SEMINOLES	T. Acted like Joe in the store
Q -21. BOOTYNY	U. Janie's weapon
J -22. MULE	V. Held the same day as Tea Cake's death
C -23. LAMP	W. Joe was the first one in Eatonville
G -24. JANIE	X. Wanted to testify at Janie's trial: ___-de-Bottom
E -25. DOG	Y. Crop they picked on the muck

MATCHING QUIZ/WORKSHEET 2 - Their Eyes Were Watching God

___ 1. JOE   A. Site of Tea Cake and Janie's wedding
___ 2. JACKSONVILLE   B. Janie's weapon
___ 3. CAKE   C. Joe made Janie wear them in the store
___ 4. HURRICANE   D. Threw his coffee cup at Coodemay
___ 5. OKECHOBEE   E. Drunken instigator of fight at the restaurant
___ 6. PHOEBY   F. Caused evacuation of the muck
___ 7. NUNKIE   G. Joe's nickname
___ 8. LAMP   H. Town celebrated its installation; street ___
___ 9. GAMBLING   I. Janie's most noticeable physical characteristic
___ 10. SIMMONS   J. How Tea Cake got Janie's money back
___ 11. RIFLE   K. Town where Joe and Janie settled
___ 12. MUCK   L. Doctor who testified in Janie's behalf
___ 13. JANIE   M. Janie brought these back from the muck
___ 14. HEADACHE   N. What Tea Cake called the Everglade crop land
___ 15. STORE   O. Janie's businessman-mayor husband
___ 16. EATONVILLE   P. Narrator of the story
___ 17. SERRENT   Q. Made a play for Tea Cake
___ 18. PISTOL   R. Raised Janie
___ 19. NANNY   S. First to hear Janie's story
___ 20. SEEDS   T. Tea ____
___ 21. BOOTYNY   U. Overflowing lake
___ 22. JODY   V. Joe started one in Eatonville
___ 23. HEADRAGS   W. Tea Cake's first symptom
___ 24. TRIAL   X. Held the same day as Tea Cake's death
___ 25. HAIR   Y. Tea Cake's weapon

KEY: MATCHING QUIZ/WORKSHEET 2 - Their Eyes Were Watching God

O - 1. JOE		A. Site of Tea Cake and Janie's wedding
A - 2. JACKSONVILLE		B. Janie's weapon
T - 3. CAKE		C. Joe made Janie wear them in the store
F - 4. HURRICANE		D. Threw his coffee cup at Coodemay
U - 5. OKECHOBEE		E. Drunken instigator of fight at the restaurant
S - 6. PHOEBY		F. Caused evacuation of the muck
Q - 7. NUNKIE		G. Joe's nickname
H - 8. LAMP		H. Town celebrated its installation; street ___
J - 9. GAMBLING		I. Janie's most noticeable physical characteristic
L -10. SIMMONS		J. How Tea Cake got Janie's money back
B -11. RIFLE		K. Town where Joe and Janie settled
N -12. MUCK		L. Doctor who testified in Janie's behalf
P -13. JANIE		M. Janie brought these back from the muck
W -14. HEADACHE		N. What Tea Cake called the Everglade crop land
V -15. STORE		O. Janie's businessman-mayor husband
K -16. EATONVILLE		P. Narrator of the story
E -17. SERRENT		Q. Made a play for Tea Cake
Y -18. PISTOL		R. Raised Janie
R -19. NANNY		S. First to hear Janie's story
M -20. SEEDS		T. Tea ___
D -21. BOOTYNY		U. Overflowing lake
G -22. JODY		V. Joe started one in Eatonville
C -23. HEADRAGS		W. Tea Cake's first symptom
X -24. TRIAL		X. Held the same day as Tea Cake's death
I -25. HAIR		Y. Tea Cake's weapon

JUGGLE LETTER REVIEW GAME CLUE SHEET - Their Eyes Were Watching God

1. AMOYR = 1. _____
   Joe was the first one in Eatonville

2. TSEOR = 2. _____
   Joe started one in Eatonville

3. OIENEMSSL = 3. _____
   Janie watched a band of them leave the muck

4. ODSOW = 4. _____
   Vergible _____; Tea Cake

5. INCRHRAUE = 5. _____
   Caused evacuation of the muck

6. AHERDSGA = 6. _____
   Joe made Janie wear them in the store

7. EDESS = 7. _____
   Janie brought these back from the muck

8. GOD = 8. _____
   Tea Cake killed it to save Janie

9. ERNRUT = 9. _____
   Mrs. ___ didn't like dark-skinned Blacks

10. NBTOOYY =10. _____
    Threw his coffee cup at Coodemay

11. DASVREGEEL =11. _____
    Location of the muck

12. OPS =12. _____
    Wanted to testify at Janie's trial: ___-de-Bottom

13. MLPA =13. _____
    Town celebrated its installation; street ___

14. EHHCAAED =14. _____
    Tea Cake's first symptom

15. SPITLO =15. _____
    Tea Cake's weapon

16. NNYNA =16. _____
Raised Janie

17. ERNSRET =17. _____
Drunken instigator of fight at the restaurant

18. CILKSKIL =18. _____
Last name of Janie's farmer husband

19. KIEZHEHA =19. _____
Acted like Joe in the store

20. LRIAT =20. _____
Held the same day as Tea Cake's death

21. KAEC =21. _____
Tea ____

22. UEML =22. _____
Nanny compared the black woman to one

23. TRMAOOBOT =23. _____
Slept through the hurricane

24. EIRBSA =24. _____
Disease Tea Cake got from dog

25. DYOJ =25. _____
Joe's nickname

26. OSSNIMM =26. _____
Doctor who testified in Janie's behalf

27. LEIFR =27. _____
Janie's weapon

28. ANEJI =28. _____
Narrator of the story

29. NLAGO =29. _____
Mr. Killicks' first name

30. ESBNA =30. _____
Crop they picked on the muck

31. ILNTVOELEA =31. _____
Town where Joe and Janie settled

32. YBHEOP   =32. _____
                            First to hear Janie's story

33. AKJENCLVLSOI   =33. _____
                            Site of Tea Cake and Janie's wedding

34. LWLAWOS   =34. _____
                            What Tea Cake couldn't do when he was sick

35. OKHEOBECE   =35. _____
                            Overflowing lake

36. OGNMIURN   =36. _____
                            It shouldn't last any longer than grief

37. IAHR   =37. _____
                            Janie's most noticeable physical characteristic

38. OJE   =38. _____
                            Janie's businessman-mayor husband

39. KMUC   =39. _____
                            What Tea Cake called the Everglade crop land

KEY: JUGGLE LETTER REVIEW GAME CLUE SHEET - Their Eyes Were Watching God

1. AMOYR = 1. MAYOR
Joe was the first one in Eatonville

2. TSEOR = 2. STORE
Joe started one in Eatonville

3. OIENEMSSL = 3. SEMINOLES
Janie watched a band of them leave the muck

4. ODSOW = 4. WOODS
Vergible _____; Tea Cake

5. INCRHRAUE = 5. HURRICANE
Caused evacuation of the muck

6. AHERDSGA = 6. HEADRAGS
Joe made Janie wear them in the store

7. EDESS = 7. SEEDS
Janie brought these back from the muck

8. GOD = 8. DOG
Tea Cake killed it to save Janie

9. ERNRUT = 9. TURNER
Mrs. ___ didn't like dark-skinned Blacks

10. NBTOOYY =10. BOOTYNY
Threw his coffee cup at Coodemay

11. DASVREGEEL =11. EVERGLADES
Location of the muck

12. OPS =12. SOP
Wanted to testify at Janie's trial: ___-de-Bottom

13. MLPA =13. LAMP
Town celebrated its installation; street ___

14. EHHCAAED =14. HEADACHE
Tea Cake's first symptom

15. SPITLO =15. PISTOL
Tea Cake's weapon

16. NNYNA =16. NANNY
Raised Janie

17. ERNSRET =17. SERRENT
Drunken instigator of fight at the restaurant

18. CILKSKIL =18. KILLICKS
Last name of Janie's farmer husband

19. KIEZHEHA =19. HEZEKIAH
Acted like Joe in the store

20. LRIAT =20. TRIAL
Held the same day as Tea Cake's death

21. KAEC =21. CAKE
Tea ____

22. UEML =22. MULE
Nanny compared the black woman to one

23. TRMAOOBOT =23. MOTORBOAT
Slept through the hurricane

24. EIRBSA =24. RABIES
Disease Tea Cake got from dog

25. DYOJ =25. JODY
Joe's nickname

26. OSSNIMM =26. SIMMONS
Doctor who testified in Janie's behalf

27. LEIFR =27. RIFLE
Janie's weapon

28. ANEJI =28. JANIE
Narrator of the story

29. NLAGO =29. LOGAN
Mr. Killicks' first name

30. ESBNA =30. BEANS
Crop they picked on the muck

31. ILNTVOELEA =31. EATONVILLE
Town where Joe and Janie settled

32. YBHEOP =32. PHOEBY
First to hear Janie's story

33. AKJENCLVLSOI =33. JACKSONVILLE
Site of Tea Cake and Janie's wedding

34. LWLAWOS =34. SWALLOW
What Tea Cake couldn't do when he was sick

35. OKHEOBECE =35. OKECHOBEE
Overflowing lake

36. OGNMIURN =36. MOURNING
It shouldn't last any longer than grief

37. IAHR =37. HAIR
Janie's most noticeable physical characteristic

38. OJE =38. JOE
Janie's businessman-mayor husband

39. KMUC =39. MUCK
What Tea Cake called the Everglade crop land

VOCABULARY RESOURCE MATERIALS

VOCABULARY WORD SEARCH *Their Eyes Were Watching God*

All the words in this list are associated with *Their Eyes Were Watching God* with an emphasis on the vocabulary words being studied in the unit. The words are placed backwards, forward, diagonally, up and

```
P R O S T R A T I N G C O B L I Q U E R
N R X W T N J R R B H V O A F E X C G E
P V O L Y E J A L E D Y N S L Z I B E P
X R E M F I E N D M A G P T M L G E L R
P E X L I M V S P U U C B O A I L D I U
R F C A O N Q I T I K U H M C I C I R S
E R R C F C E E D R S F Q E T R Y L C U
D A U E E G I N J I L E S U R L I O A B
E C C R N A J T C L U T F U T O D T S M
C T I A D P G S Y E S I S N L N U S E I
E E A T Z E Q A J D T D A U U T D S U S
S D T I N D F C L K I L P O L E R W L S
S H I N O T N A W N L V P K W L N Y O I
O H N G M P V R S A Y X S O D D E N G O
R Z G B Y Z P F G D E H C A O R B N Y N
```

BROACHED	FETID	LANGUID	REFRACTED	TRANSIENTS
COSMIC	FIEND	LUSTILY	SACRILEGE	TREACHEROUS
COWED	FRACAS	MALICE	SODDEN	USURPER
DELIRIUM	FUTILE	MIEN	STOLID	VELOCITY
EULOGY	GALLANTLY	OBLIQUE	SUBMISSION	WANTON
EXCRUCIATING	GAPED	PREDECESSOR	SUBTLE	
EXPOUND	HYPOCRITES	PROMINENCE	SULLEN	
FEND	LACERATING	PROSTRATING	SULTRY	

VOCABULARY WORD SEARCH ANSWER KEY
Their Eyes Were Watching God

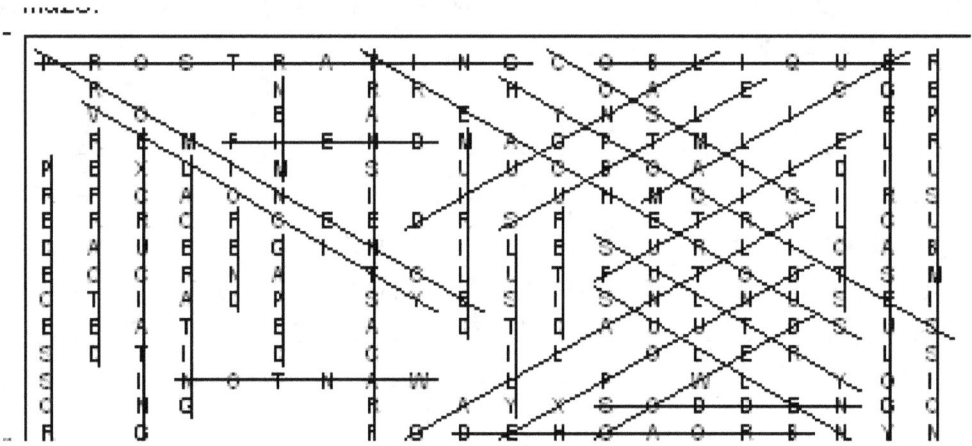

144

VOCABULARY CROSSWORD *Their Eyes Were Watching God*

VOCABULARY CROSSWORD CLUES *Their Eyes Were Watching God*

ACROSS
1. Guesses
4. Ill-will
8. Unavoidable
9. Hot and humid
13. Intensely painful
17. Released
18. Held open
19. Widely known
20. Unresisting acceptance

DOWN
2. Slanting
3. Emotionless
5. Robustly
6. Merciless
7. Offensive odor
10. Cutting; tearing
11. Dangerous
12. Bad or evil person
14. Long lasting
15. Resist
16. Teasing

VOCABULARY CROSSWORD ANSWER KEY
Their Eyes Were Watching God

Across: CONJECTURES, MALICE, INEVITABLE, SULTRY, EXCRUCIATING, DISENGAGED, GAPED, PROMINENCE, RESIGNATION

Down: OBLIQUE, STOLID, MUSTILY, ACCRATING (ACCELERATING), TREACHERE, FEIGNED, WINTO, BLE, FETID, ENDURABLE

VOCABULARY WORKSHEET 1 - Their Eyes Were Watching God

___ 1. DWINDLED   A. Speed
___ 2. BAITING   B. Nobly; boldy
___ 3. CONSOLIDATED   C. Explain; give a detailed account
___ 4. SUBTLE   D. Plea; earnest request
___ 5. OBLIQUE   E. Universal; vast
___ 6. LANGUID   F. Having little or no emotion
___ 7. TREACHEROUS   G. Unbelieving; skeptical
___ 8. PERSEVERANCE   H. Slanted
___ 9. VELOCITY   I. Against something sacred
___10. COSMIC   J. United into one system; combined
___11. DISGORGED   K. Became gradually smaller until nothing remained
___12. SODDEN   L. Sulky; morose
___13. PROMINENCE   M. Lacking energy or vitality; weak
___14. INCREDULOUS   N. Dangerous
___15. SUPPLICATION   O. Bullied
___16. COWED   P. Difficult to detect
___17. SACRILEGE   Q. Strolled
___18. PUGNACIOUSLY   R. Persistence; dogged trying
___19. DELIRIUM   S. Giving in to another
___20. EXPOUND   T. Vomited; threw up
___21. STOLID   U. Taunting, teasing, luring
___22. SAUNTERED   V. Widely known; being easily identified
___23. GALLANTLY   W. Combative in nature; belligerently; rebelliously
___24. SULLEN   X. Soaked; saturated
___25. SUBMISSION   Y. Mental confusion caused by illness

KEY: VOCABULARY WORKSHEET 1 - Their Eyes Were Watching God

K - 1.	DWINDLED	A. Speed
U - 2.	BAITING	B. Nobly; boldy
J - 3.	CONSOLIDATED	C. Explain; give a detailed account
P - 4.	SUBTLE	D. Plea; earnest request
H - 5.	OBLIQUE	E. Universal; vast
M - 6.	LANGUID	F. Having little or no emotion
N - 7.	TREACHEROUS	G. Unbelieving; skeptical
R - 8.	PERSEVERANCE	H. Slanted
A - 9.	VELOCITY	I. Against something sacred
E - 10.	COSMIC	J. United into one system; combined
T - 11.	DISGORGED	K. Became gradually smaller until nothing remained
X - 12.	SODDEN	L. Sulky; morose
V - 13.	PROMINENCE	M. Lacking energy or vitality; weak
G - 14.	INCREDULOUS	N. Dangerous
D - 15.	SUPPLICATION	O. Bullied
O - 16.	COWED	P. Difficult to detect
I - 17.	SACRILEGE	Q. Strolled
W 18.	PUGNACIOUSLY	R. Persistence; dogged trying
Y - 19.	DELIRIUM	S. Giving in to another
C - 20.	EXPOUND	T. Vomited; threw up
F - 21.	STOLID	U. Taunting, teasing, luring
Q - 22.	SAUNTERED	V. Widely known; being easily identified
B - 23.	GALLANTLY	W. Combative in nature; belligerently; rebelliously
L - 24.	SULLEN	X. Soaked; saturated
S - 25.	SUBMISSION	Y. Mental confusion caused by illness

VOCABULARY WORKSHEET 2 - Their Eyes Were Watching God

___ 1. GALLANTLY   A. Dangerous

___ 2. PROMINENCE   B. Widely known; being easily identified

___ 3. LUSTILY   C. Vomited; threw up

___ 4. MALICE   D. Area of control or power

___ 5. FIEND   E. A fight; a brawl

___ 6. PROSTRATING   F. Robustly; strongly

___ 7. SULTRY   G. An ancestor; one who came before

___ 8. INSINUATIONS   H. Very hot and humid

___ 9. PUGNACIOUSLY   I. Nobly; boldy

___ 10. EXCRUCIATING   J. Combative in nature; belligerently; rebelliously

___ 11. PREDECESSOR   K. Wasted away; weakened

___ 12. FEROCITY   L. Extreme ill-will or spite

___ 13. DISGORGED   M. Unresisting acceptance

___ 14. COSMIC   N. Bowing down in adoration or submission

___ 15. TREACHEROUS   O. Able to be tolerated for a long time

___ 16. COWED   P. Savageness; fierceness

___ 17. RESIGNATION   Q. Unavoidable

___ 18. USURPER   R. Bad or evil person

___ 19. FRACAS   S. Subtly made suggestions

___ 20. ENDURABLE   T. Bullied

___ 21. INEVITABLE   U. Lacking energy or vitality; weak

___ 22. LANGUISHED   V. Universal; vast

___ 23. JURISDICTION   W. Intensely painful; agonizing

___ 24. COMPELLMENT   X. Strong urging forces

___ 25. LANGUID   Y. One who grabs money or property

KEY: VOCABULARY WORKSHEET 2 - Their Eyes Were Watching God

I - 1.	GALLANTLY	A. Dangerous
B - 2.	PROMINENCE	B. Widely known; being easily identified
F - 3.	LUSTILY	C. Vomited; threw up
L - 4.	MALICE	D. Area of control or power
R - 5.	FIEND	E. A fight; a brawl
N - 6.	PROSTRATING	F. Robustly; strongly
H - 7.	SULTRY	G. An ancestor; one who came before
S - 8.	INSINUATIONS	H. Very hot and humid
J - 9.	PUGNACIOUSLY	I. Nobly; boldy
W - 10.	EXCRUCIATING	J. Combative in nature; belligerently; rebelliously
G - 11.	PREDECESSOR	K. Wasted away; weakened
P - 12.	FEROCITY	L. Extreme ill-will or spite
C - 13.	DISGORGED	M. Unresisting acceptance
V - 14.	COSMIC	N. Bowing down in adoration or submission
A - 15.	TREACHEROUS	O. Able to be tolerated for a long time
T - 16.	COWED	P. Savageness; fierceness
M - 17.	RESIGNATION	Q. Unavoidable
Y - 18.	USURPER	R. Bad or evil person
E - 19.	FRACAS	S. Subtly made suggestions
O - 20.	ENDURABLE	T. Bullied
Q - 21.	INEVITABLE	U. Lacking energy or vitality; weak
K - 22.	LANGUISHED	V. Universal; vast
D - 23.	JURISDICTION	W. Intensely painful; agonizing
X - 24.	COMPELLMENT	X. Strong urging forces
U - 25.	LANGUID	Y. One who grabs money or property

VOCABULARY JUGGLE LETTER REVIEW GAME CLUE SHEET 1 - Their Eyes Were Watching God

1. TOLISD = 1. _____
Having little or no emotion

2. ASIIRNTGONE = 2. _____
Unresisting acceptance

3. IRDEDGSOG = 3. _____
Vomited; threw up

4. NEMI = 4. _____
Manner or appearance

5. EIEMDPZORT = 5. _____
Negotiated to gain time

6. EFLTUI = 6. _____
Having no useful result

7. SEEODPRESRC = 7. _____
An ancestor; one who came before

8. SYILAUUNCGOP = 8. _____
Combative in nature; belligerently; rebelliously

9. IIDURMLE = 9. _____
Mental confusion caused by illness

10. TLYALANLG =10. _____
Nobly; boldy

11. ENEALBURD =11. _____
Able to be tolerated for a long time

12. EDNSDO =12. _____
Soaked; saturated

13. SOTACRUREHE =13. _____
Dangerous

14. ERFERDATC =14. _____
Deflected from a straight path

15. UXOEPND =15. _____
Explain; give a detailed account

16. RCIELSEAG   =16. _____
                       Against something sacred

17. GEDGDSEAIN   =17. _____
                       Released; detached

18. OFEITYCR   =18. _____
                       Savageness; fierceness

19. ECWOD   =19. _____
                       Bullied

20. UPLAICOSNIPT =20. _____
                       Plea; earnest request

21. RESUNEATD   =21. _____
                       Strolled

22. LLSUTYI   =22. _____
                       Robustly; strongly

23. IUSNNAOINSIT =23. _____
                       Subtly made suggestions

24. AGDLINU   =24. _____
                       Lacking energy or vitality; weak

25. ELWDDIDN   =25. _____
                       Became gradually smaller until nothing remained

26. ERNUSULIODC   =26. _____
                       Unbelieving; skeptical

27. PERENARCSEEV =27. _____
                       Persistence; dogged trying

KEY: VOCAB. JUGGLE LETTER REVIEW GAME CLUE SHEET 1 - Their Eyes Were Watching God

1. TOLISD = 1. STOLID
   Having little or no emotion

2. ASIIRNTGONE = 2. RESIGNATION
   Unresisting acceptance

3. IRDEDGSOG = 3. DISGORGED
   Vomited; threw up

4. NEMI = 4. MIEN
   Manner or appearance

5. EIEMDPZORT = 5. TEMPORIZED
   Negotiated to gain time

6. EFLTUI = 6. FUTILE
   Having no useful result

7. SEEODPRESRC = 7. PREDECESSOR
   An ancestor; one who came before

8. SYILAUUNCGOP = 8. PUGNACIOUSLY
   Combative in nature; belligerently; rebelliously

9. IIDURMLE = 9. DELIRIUM
   Mental confusion caused by illness

10. TLYALANLG = 10. GALLANTLY
    Nobly; boldy

11. ENEALBRUD = 11. ENDURABLE
    Able to be tolerated for a long time

12. EDNSDO = 12. SODDEN
    Soaked; saturated

13. SOTACRUREHE = 13. TREACHEROUS
    Dangerous

14. ERFERDATC = 14. REFRACTED
    Deflected from a straight path

15. UXOEPND = 15. EXPOUND
    Explain; give a detailed account

16. RCIELSEAG = 16. SACRILEGE
Against something sacred

17. GEDGDSEAIN = 17. DISENGAGED
Released; detached

18. OFEITYCR = 18. FEROCITY
Savageness; fierceness

19. ECWOD = 19. COWED
Bullied

20. UPLAICOSNIPT = 20. SUPPLICATION
Plea; earnest request

21. RESUNEATD = 21. SAUNTERED
Strolled

22. LLSUTYI = 22. LUSTILY
Robustly; strongly

23. IUSNNAOINSIT = 23. INSINUATIONS
Subtly made suggestions

24. AGDLINU = 24. LANGUID
Lacking energy or vitality; weak

25. ELWDDIDN = 25. DWINDLED
Became gradually smaller until nothing remained

26. ERNUSULIODC = 26. INCREDULOUS
Unbelieving; skeptical

27. PERENARCSEEV = 27. PERSEVERANCE
Persistence; dogged trying

VOCABULARY JUGGLE LETTER REVIEW GAME CLUE SHEET 2 - Their Eyes Were Watching God

1. GEYOUL = 1. _____
   Speech or praise about a dead person

2. EAGPD = 2. _____
   Opened wide

3. UPREUSR = 3. _____
   One who grabs money or property

4. NALCGIAETR = 4. _____
   Ripping; cutting; tearing

5. ROSUNDCITJII = 5. _____
   Area of control or power

6. RSYTUL = 6. _____
   Very hot and humid

7. LMEOCTEPNML = 7. _____
   Strong urging forces

8. NSOIUBSSIM = 8. _____
   Giving in to another

9. NOIDSDTACLEO = 9. _____
   United into one system; combined

10. RSTAGIDCEEN =10. _____
    Violating the sacredness of

11. NEFD =11. _____
    Resist; push away

12. INFDE =12. _____
    Bad or evil person

13. SLHUEDNGIA =13. _____
    Wasted away; weakened

14. TRHIPCYEOS =14. _____
    People who say one thing but do the opposite

15. NAIBIGT =15. _____
    Taunting, teasing, luring

16. USNOTJECCER =16. _____
Ideas formed from guessing

17. ONTAWN =17. _____
Cruel; merciless

18. ICSMOC =18. _____
Universal; vast

19. ANCECIUTIXGR =19. _____
Intensely painful; agonizing

20. LNULSE =20. _____
Sulky; morose

21. CIMELA =21. _____
Extreme ill-will or spite

22. YOCVLETI =22. _____
Speed

23. DTFEI =23. _____
Having an offensive odor

24. BILEVAINTE =24. _____
Unavoidable

25. TANSNIRTSE =25. _____
People without permanent homes

26. ASRPNGIROTT =26. _____
Bowing down in adoration or submission

27. UIOEQLB =27. _____
Slanted

KEY: VOCAB. JUGGLE LETTER REVIEW GAME CLUE SHEET 2 - Their Eyes Were Watching God

1. GEYOUL = 1. EULOGY
   Speech or praise about a dead person

2. EAGPD = 2. GAPED
   Opened wide

3. UPREUSR = 3. USURPER
   One who grabs money or property

4. NALCGIAETR = 4. LACERATING
   Ripping; cutting; tearing

5. ROSUNDCITJII = 5. JURISDICTION
   Area of control or power

6. RSYTUL = 6. SULTRY
   Very hot and humid

7. LMEOCTEPNML = 7. COMPELLMENT
   Strong urging forces

8. NSOIUBSSIM = 8. SUBMISSION
   Giving in to another

9. NOIDSDTACLEO = 9. CONSOLIDATED
   United into one system; combined

10. RSTAGIDCEEN =10. DESECRATING
    Violating the sacredness of

11. NEFD =11. FEND
    Resist; push away

12. INFDE =12. FIEND
    Bad or evil person

13. SLHUEDNGIA =13. LANGUISHED
    Wasted away; weakened

14. TRHIPCYEOS =14. HYPOCRITES
    People who say one thing but do the opposite

15. NAIBIGT =15. BAITING
    Taunting, teasing, luring

16. USNOTJECCER =16. CONJECTURES
Ideas formed from guessing

17. ONTAWN =17. WANTON
Cruel; merciless

18. ICSMOC =18. COSMIC
Universal; vast

19. ANCECIUTIXGR =19. EXCRUCIATING
Intensely painful; agonizing

20. LNULSE =20. SULLEN
Sulky; morose

21. CIMELA =21. MALICE
Extreme ill-will or spite

22. YOCVLETI =22. VELOCITY
Speed

23. DTFEI =23. FETID
Having an offensive odor

24. BILEVAINTE =24. INEVITABLE
Unavoidable

25. TANSNIRTSE =25. TRANSIENTS
People without permanent homes

26. ASRPNGIROTT =26. PROSTRATING
Bowing down in adoration or submission

27. UIOEQLB =27. OBLIQUE
Slanted

www.ingramcontent.com/pod-product-compliance
Lightning Source LLC
Chambersburg PA
CBHW051410070526
44584CB00023B/3362